APPEARANCE OBSESSION

Learning To Love The Way You Look

Joni E. Johnston, Psy. D.

Health Communications, Inc.
Deerfield Beach, Florida

Library of Congress Cataloging-in-Publication Data

Johnston, Joni E.
    Appearance obsession: learning to love the way you look/Joni E.
Johnston.
      p.   cm.
    ISBN 1-55874-270-0: $9.95
    1. Body image. 2. Body, Human — Social aspects. 3. Beauty. Per-
sonal — Psychological aspects. 4. Self-esteem. I. Title.
BF697.5.B63J64   1993   93-46941
158'.1—dc20   CIP

© 1994 Joni E. Johnston
ISBN 1-55874-270-0

Publisher: Health Communications, Inc.
               3201 S.W. 15th Street
               Deerfield Beach, Florida 33442-8190

Cover design by Andrea Perrine Brower

Dedicated To Two of My Cornerstones
Alex Tsakiris
and
Margaret Peterson

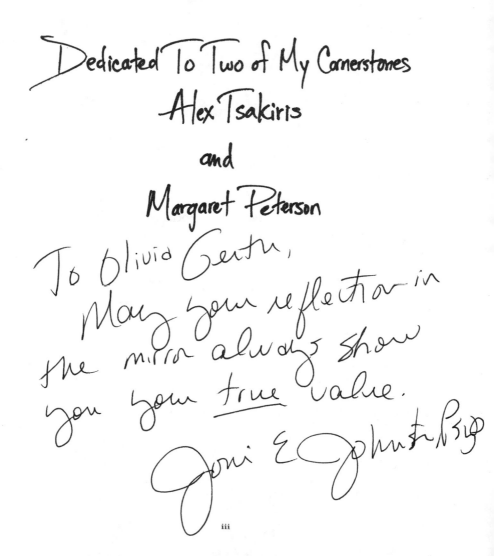

To Olivia Gerth,
May your reflection in
the mirror always show
you your _true_ value.
Joni E Johnston PsyD

iii

ACKNOWLEDGMENTS

As I write these acknowledgments, I am struck by a feeling I often have when I am leaving for a trip. As I'm heading for the airport, a voice inside my head starts reviewing the contents of my suitcase. "Do you have your airplane ticket? Did you remember your toothbrush? What are you forgetting?"

Of course, I can always buy a new toothbrush when I get to where I'm going. I could never, however, replace the help, support and encouragement I have received from the people listed below. Without them this book would never have happened.

For the development and production of this book, I feel a deep sense of gratitude:

- to my literary agent, Evan Fogelman, for his energy, enthusiasm, and unwavering faith in me
- to Linda Diehl, for her dependability and professionalism
- to Barbara Nichols at Health Communications, Inc., for believing in this book's message and to Naomi Lucks for her fine editing
- to Christi Watson, for her hours as a volunteer survey collector and for always going beyond the call of duty
- to my statistician, John Bassler, for his ongoing patience and assistance

- to Sara Hays, for her editorial review and for wonderful Friday mornings
- to my mentor, Suzanne Boswell, for her business savvy and unwavering support
- to Cynthia Morris, for more things than I could possibly list here
- to Janeice Weinand for her help with data collection
- to my sister, Julie, for always being there
- to my partner, Sara Adams, for her friendship over the years
- to Nana, for her unconditional love
- to my mom, for always doing the best she could and for doing so many things right
- and to my husband, Alex, for listening, reading, editing, supporting, loving and most of all for just being you.

CONTENTS

PRETTY BABY BLUES

"Ladies and gentleman, Miss America of 1980 has just been born." My father loved to tell me this story. As a professional baseball player in his early twenties, he had been on the road the day I was born. My grandmother had called a friend, who had gone to the baseball stadium to tell my dad. And the baseball announcer, upon hearing the news, had promptly proclaimed the emergence of a new beauty queen, one of the highest compliments a girl could receive in 1960.

Telling me that story was a way for my dad to communicate how beautiful and special he thought I was. But I always had mixed feelings — some of the same feelings, in fact, that I have struggled with much of my adult life.

Although the announcer certainly had exaggerated, I did receive considerable attention for my appearance as a child. Strangers would frequently comment on how "cute" I was. My mother always seemed so proud of me whenever I was complimented.

My grandmother frequently told me how pretty I was. My aunt also focused on my looks; I'll never forget how angry she was when, at age seven, I was chosen first runner-up in a local beauty pageant. I felt so ashamed that I had disappointed her by not winning the contest. The unfavorable comments she made about the winner, a schoolmate and friend of mine, were confusing and frightening, but I certainly enjoyed my parents' attention that night.

I remember watching beauty contests on TV at an early age. The women were so beautiful and slim. The crowd seemed to adore the winner, and her crown sparkled. I used to daydream sometimes about winning a contest and waltzing down the aisle to the tune of "Miss America." At the age of five, I didn't understand why I couldn't go into the locker room with my brother to see my dad after a baseball game. Watching the beauty contests, though, I learned that there were places where girls were special and boys were "not allowed."

My most painful childhood memories related to appearance had to do with my weight. While I received praise for my facial features, my large appetite as a child was a matter of considerable concern to my mother, who seemed constantly afraid that I would get fat. She was well acquainted with the negative social consequences associated with obesity, and struggled with her own issues about weight and appearance. She channeled her anxiety into action with an attempt to help me control my appetite by frequently pointing out fattening foods or commenting on the "excess" amount of food I was eating.

In my family, rules about food were different for boys and girls. Second portions were intended for my dad and my brother. Although my mother usually sat at the table with us, she ate very little during dinnertime. Yet I would sometimes see her eating junk food alone, after we were supposed to be in bed. Although my mother never had a weight problem, she seemed preoccupied with her weight. Even as a child, I knew how important it was to my mother to be thin. I knew the right answer when she asked me if I thought she had gained weight, since I could see how upsetting this possibility was to her.

I felt guilty whenever I ate more than I knew I "should." I remember occasionally sneaking food out of the refrigerator.

Once I lied to my mother about how much I had eaten after coming home from ballet lessons. I believed something was wrong with me because I enjoyed eating so much.

My grandmother, on the other hand, provided love through food. One of our favorite rituals when I was spending the night with her was going to the grocery store and stocking up on any and every food I selected. With every childhood illness came a fruit basket, an assortment of fruit, candy and gum that my grandmother lovingly selected in the hope that it would make me feel better. While she was quick to comment any time she thought my mother had gained weight, a criticism that would darken my mother's mood for hours, she indulged me. At an early age, eating became a symbol of many different and conflicting things for me — comfort, pleasure, a lack of self-control. As I got older, I recognized many of these same mixed messages in various magazines and media sources.

In spite of the generally positive attention I received about my appearance, or maybe partly because of the self-consciousness that resulted, I did not think I was attractive enough as a child. First runner-up meant failure to me. Frequent encouragement to dress a certain way, or reminders of how pretty I looked only when my hair was combed, relayed the message that my looks changed depending on my clothes or grooming. Pictures of my mother as a child reminded me that she was a lot thinner at that age than I was. I remember sitting at a pool when I was about eight years old and suddenly feeling embarrassed as I noticed my stomach protruding over my two-piece bathing suit.

To this day I am surprised when looking back at childhood pictures; they reveal a child of average height and weight. The child I knew looked a lot different. She had fat legs, "chipmunk cheeks" and a chubby stomach.

In spite of my own somewhat confused view of my looks, grade school taught me the benefits of others perceiving me as attractive. Teachers seemed to pay more attention to the good-looking kids. They seemed to like us more. I was lucky and I knew it — in fact, I felt guilty about it. It didn't seem fair to me that I would get extra attention because other people thought I was "cute"; I didn't have any control over my appearance and neither did the unattractive kids. Sometimes I tried to make up for my special treatment by being extra nice to the less popular kids. Sometimes I rebelled against any focus on my appearance; my grandmother laughingly tells stories of chasing me around the room in order to comb my hair. At other times I just enjoyed my good fortune.

By preadolescence, that awkward period between childhood and puberty, I was still painfully self-conscious about my own appearance but I was no longer ambivalent about my desire to fit in. I had begun to read fashion magazines and observe the women promoted by the media as examples of beauty. Quickly learning that blondes had more fun, and observing the preponderance of towheaded models and beauty contestants, my brown hair suddenly became a challenge to overcome.

A friend and I spent the better part of a fifth-grade afternoon bleaching our hair with Sun-In. Thus I became the only girl in my fifth-grade class to have dark roots accompanied by orange hair. Although the horrifying results and painful teasing from family members cured me of future hair experiments, a pattern of trying to improve my looks so I would feel better about my appearance had begun.

At about age 14, puberty kicked in and my body thinned and lengthened in a dramatically short time. Even more startling, boys abruptly began to notice me. The same boys who had been indifferent to me even three months before were now giving me the eye. Like most teenagers I compared myself regularly to my girlfriends in an attempt to get some kind of assessment of how I was progressing in my physical development. I especially noticed my friends with developing breasts, as that part of my anatomy did not seem to be keeping up with the changes taking place in the rest of my body. At age 16, I decided to get breast enhancement surgery if by age 25 I had not developed them on my own.

I am convinced that a combination of close friends, certain social events and "thin genes" saved me from an eating disorder during adolescence. Bombarded with thin fashion/role models from the outside, and confusion about my rapidly changing appearance from within, I looked more and more to outside sources for affirmation about how I looked. Luckily for me the outside confirmation was there — long enough, at least, to get me safely through high school.

In the southern town where I grew up, traditional stereotypes of women and men were exaggerated. Local beauty pageants were well-publicized events, and to be Homecoming Queen for the local high school brought instant notoriety. For females, being beautiful still carried a lot more weight than being smart, in spite of the slowly changing roles for men and women. In my town women seemed either plain and smart or beautiful and dumb. I was told countless times that I was "too pretty to be so smart," a statement that was confusingly complimentary.

Here I was: being elected "most attractive" of my class and school beauty; representing the football team as its queen at Homecoming; winning local beauty contests and qualifying for state beauty pageants. And all the while I was becoming increasingly confused and distressed by the discrepancy between how I saw myself and how others seemed to see me.

I didn't look like Cybill Shepherd, the 17-year-old winner of the Model of the Year contest. She was willowy thin and had a perfectly chiseled nose and a small mouth. When I looked in the mirror, I saw thunder thighs, a pug nose and a round face. I was sure Cybill never lost control and pigged out on an entire bag of pretzels, or ate more than her boyfriend at the local Mexican restaurant.

I can barely describe the myriad feelings I had during my high school years. I loved the attention and the temporary respite each honor gave me from my appearance insecurity. I felt guilty for receiving attention for something that I had done nothing to earn. I was confused that there seemed to be so many more attractive girls, yet I was chosen as the most appealing. I was even more confused that something as random as looks could be given so much emphasis. Perhaps most difficult of all, I felt significant pressure to look as good as I could and to be as nice as I could so that I might somehow feel worthy of all this recognition.

Nothing seemed to permanently improve my painful relationship with my appearance. Receiving compliments from others or a beauty honor provided a short-lived boost — just like buying a new outfit temporarily compensated for a negative body image. As soon as the newness of these external events wore off, my appearance insecurity resurfaced.

Participating in a couple of state beauty pageants exposed me
to new realities. I was amazed at the seriousness with which
some of the contestants competed. For many of the girls, the
contest represented not only new opportunities, but the sole way
out of a limited future. I have read about cutthroat interactions
among competitors, but I never encountered this during my limited days of beauty pageant involvement. Rather, the casualties
seemed to be some of the girls themselves, as evidenced by their
obsessive diet patterns and beauty routines, and in the excruciat-
ingly critical way they assessed every facial feature and body
part. Girls traded Mark Eden bust developers and worried about
the tiniest weight gain.

All families, to varying extents, mirror societal values and standards. My parents' personal history of physical attractiveness and
its accompanying social rewards, plus the increasing focus on beauty in the media, perpetuated a strong emphasis on physical attractiveness among members of my family. This was particularly true
among the women.

When I was a teenager, the power of feminine beauty and the
importance of appearance maintenance were communicated to
me in a number of ways. Once they reached a certain age, girls
should never go out in public, even to the grocery store, without
wearing makeup. New clothes were of crucial importance at significant social events. Happiness meant losing a few pounds, and
staying thin meant you were self-controlled and disciplined.

Luckily my family's emphasis on education and intellectual pur-
suits provided some balance to their unique version of conformity
to societal beauty standards. Since my mother and grandmother
were schoolteachers, and many of my relatives had obtained de-
grees at a time when it was relatively rare, my family, particularly
my mother's side, placed a premium on education. I received consistent praise and encouragement whenever I showed an interest
in learning. "You're smart" was a message communicated to me
at an early age, and my family's unwavering confidence in my
ability to succeed provided a firm foundation for achievement.

While this did not reduce the pressure I felt with regard to
appearance demands, I at least had another way to feel good about
certain parts of myself. Unlike most aspects of my physical appearance, intellectual accomplishments were something I could control

through effort. I could make A's if I studied. I could take care of myself financially if I got a good job. If beauty standards had been my only measure of self-worth, I can only imagine the helplessness I would have felt. Seeing the frantic competition of some of the beauty contestants had certainly awakened me to that reality.

Prior to college my appearance obsession consisted primarily of painful thoughts and feelings about my looks, feelings of self-consciousness and insecurity that surfaced repeatedly during my teenage years. Looking back I realize that even then I had begun to rely on fashion as a security blanket. However, during adolescence my body fit the beauty standards. I was tall and thin; a fast metabolism and regular exercise as a tennis team member and drill team participant allowed me to eat to my heart's content. Dieting and appearance-related exercise were not necessary.

My love/hate affair with dieting and exercise began at age 19. I spent my first year of college gaining the amount of weight most college students seemed to gain, the "freshman 15." Given complete freedom of choice over my diet, I ate double-cheeseburgers and French fries for breakfast for three months. Exams signaled late-night pizza binges with my roommate, with an occasional banana split thrown in to celebrate their completion.

In addition, when I entered college, my drill team days were over. I was no longer physically active. The fitness craze was just hitting the Auburn campus and I began to see female classmates jogging. Aerobics articles were appearing in women's magazines. The appearance stakes had increased; no longer could you just be thin, now you had to be toned and well-defined. In my eyes beautiful girls with "perfect" bodies were everywhere.

Continuing a pattern that had begun in adolescence, my college boyfriend was extremely good-looking. Dating handsome men seemed to be another way to prove to myself that I was attractive. If this handsome guy was interested in me, then I must be good-looking too, right? This line of reasoning was completely ineffective and ultimately created more tension. Since I relied on this person's attractiveness to somehow confirm my own, I naturally reasoned that he was significantly more appealing than I was. I knew this, thought everyone else knew this and was convinced that it was only a matter of time before he realized it and moved on.

Other aspects of my self were much more solid. A bad grade did not mean that I was dumb. A quarrel with a friend did not mean that I was a "social zero" or a bad person. I could challenge a professor on a point in class and feel confident in my opinion.

Yet an unflattering angle in the mirror invoked feelings of disgust. An innocent remark from my boyfriend about an attractive woman triggered alarm signals. Articles touting the latest diets or exercise regimens inspired temporary motivation and enthusiam, fizzling into guilt and recriminations when I failed to be consistent.

Nutrition and exercise were not about health, they were about looking good. My roommate Angie and I embarked on many weight loss and exercise journeys together. We ate a week's worth of Scarsdale diet food in one day. We tried the banana, egg and hot dog diet. We religiously ran/walked around the inside track of the basketball stadium for a few days and then abruptly gave up. We alternately provided motivation and excuses for each other. We gained weight, we lost it, we overate and we underate.

I shared none of this struggle with my boyfriend: if he knew how unhappy I was with my appearance, he would really see how unattractive I was! Part of my appearance insecurity manifested itself in a need to at least act as if I felt good about the way I looked. While at times I was unable to refrain from pulling for reassurance from my partner, for the most part I hid my insecurities well. I never verbalized the agonizing comparisons I made between myself and other attractive women. I accepted compliments, although I didn't believe them. I never made negative comments about my body, and hoped that he wouldn't notice the cellulite camping on the back of my thighs.

In between frantic attempts to improve my appearance, I distracted myself by focusing on my grades and pending application to graduate school. Graduate school itself was a temporary reprieve, at least in terms of my painful obsession about my appearance. Ironically, while I had spent the last two years of college attempting and failing to rid myself of the "freshman 15," I lost 25 pounds during my first semester of graduate school. My diet formula was full-time school, full-time waitressing, cigarette smoking and late-night coffee drinking.

I was so busy during my first semester that, for the first time in my life, I would forget to eat. It was also the first time since early childhood that I was virtually unaware of my appearance. I would occasionally go to class in jeans and my pajama shirt. I never watched TV and "light reading" meant a chapter in my favorite school textbook. I was literally unexposed to popular media sources. I felt stress over school demands, yet these freed me from the pressure of worrying about my appearance.

When I returned home for Christmas, my friends and family were shocked over my dramatic weight loss. I remember constant admonishments to eat, and caring attempts to criticize me into weight gain. "You don't look good, you're too thin, look at those arms, they look like toothpicks," were frequent remarks. I had never received feedback for being "too thin," so after my chubby college days these statements to me were words of encouragement. I had not lost the weight intentionally; in fact, until I returned home, I don't think I realized how much weight I had dropped. Getting attention for being so thin, though, created a new appreciation for my reduced figure. I became determined to keep it at all costs.

That Christmas I began an eight-year obsession with weight maintenance. I lived in fear of relapsing into my undergraduate body. I was not anorexic in the sense that I did not want to keep losing weight, nor did I see myself as "fat." I do admit to a certain satisfaction when I lost one or two pounds during my attempts at weight control. These lost pounds did not mean that I looked better, but meant that I had more "insurance" against regaining the weight that I had lost. Even though I continued to get feedback that I was "too thin," I was afraid to go back to even my high school weight, as any weight gain to me symbolized a loss of control and pending obesity.

Because my body was below its natural set-point, I initially needed tremendous effort to keep the weight off. What's more, I had adjusted to the rigorous graduate school schedule and my eating habits had adjusted as well. My renewed appetite made it really hard to stick to my newly imposed weight-control schedule.

I weighed myself four or five times a week. I knew how many calories chewing gum had in it. I rigidly compensated for any slight overindulgence by cutting back the following day. I began a

rigid exercise program and took a training class to be an instructor, but had to quit due to an injury. Keeping my body below
normal weight and exercising vigorously gave me a sense of control and accomplishment. While I continued to view my body as
an object to be molded rather than appreciated, at least I was
winning the battle.

My adversarial relationship with my body didn't seem to be
much different than that experienced by most of the women I
exercised with. I heard many locker-room stories of dieting and
exercise. Few of the aerobics participants actually seemed to enjoy
the exercise; rather it seemed to be a necessary chore with a
socially rewarded outcome. These weren't women with "eating
disorders"; these were women who were trying to "be beautiful."

We all heard murmurings of exercise mates who had crossed
the line between applauded discipline and "clinical pathology." I'll
never forget my first encounter with a woman I later realized
was anorexic. Still in the early days of graduate school, I knew
next to nothing about anorexia nervosa. I remember seeing an
emaciated young woman worshipfully aerobicizing with weights
that were heavier than her arms seemed to be. The look on her
face was orgasmic. She seemed unaware of her surroundings and
completely engrossed in her activity. I didn't know exactly why I
felt so uncomfortable watching her. Was it my clinical intuition
telling me something was drastically wrong, or the recognition
that she and I were similar in our goals if not our methods?

From age 21 to 27 I channeled my appearance obsession into
strict diet and exercise. I certainly managed to lead a life during
this time; I married, moved to Chicago, received my doctorate
and moved to Dallas. With each change came a temporary esca-
lation both in my self-consciousness about my appearance and in
the rigid ways I attempted to improve and control my looks.

Feeling overwhelmed by the adjustment to a new spouse, a
new city and an internship, I spent the first year of my marriage
dieting vigorously during the week and splurging on the weekend.
I nurtured myself through homemade cookies, Chex mix and
Pizzaria Uno pizza. During the week I jogged daily and kept a
running tab of every calorie I ate. I saved calories during the week
so I could indulge on Saturday and Sunday.

I was completely unaware that I was on the verge of bulimia. I was not using laxatives or diet pills. I was not vomiting in order to get rid of food. My weight never varied more than two or three pounds. I exercised regularly but not excessively. I did not secretly consume large amounts of food. These were the symptoms I associated with a serious problem with food. Yet my ongoing pattern of strict dieting followed by overindulgence closely resembled the binge/purge cycle I became familiar with through clients after I entered private practice.

Sure I thought about food a lot. I often daydreamed about my "weekend" foods, foods that were strictly off limits during my diet-conscious week. It never occurred to me that my week of deprivation might actually be causing my weekend sprees. Instead, I secretly viewed myself, and my indulgent weekend eating habits, as the "real" me, the one that would easily trick me into dramatic weight gain should my ironclad control fail me.

Yes, I dieted regularly, didn't most women? I had trouble believing I was "thin enough," and knew I tended to overestimate my body parts. So did most of my friends, regardless of their actual body size.

The compliments I frequently received for my body size surely made the weekly battle worth it. Being told I looked "like a model" was the next best thing to being one of the selected few on the magazine covers. My husband never made any negative comments about my appearance; he was extremely tolerant of my unusual eating habits and never encouraged or discouraged me about exercise. He occasionally teased me about my self-consciousness and my periodic reliance on clothes in social situations. Being a man of the eighties, he also made it clear that he liked my thin, well-exercised form. And as the media began to tout a male ideal that was strong and muscular, and bodybuilding for appearance emerged, he began to experience pressure about his appearance as well.

There is no doubt that actually being thin did help my perception of my appearance to some degree. Getting consistent positive feedback about my body size gradually sank in over the years. While I could not see this thin person in the mirror, I did come to believe that this was how other people saw me. Yet it just wasn't enough. My perceived body size changed with my mood or social environment.

Compliments did not erase my dissatisfaction with my overall appearance. I still saw a pug nose, a flat chest and a large mouth. My ways of coping with my painful feelings about my looks — through dieting, shopping and exercise — at least allowed me for the first time to believe that I could do something about my appearance insecurity. I did things that were socially sanctioned and that gave me a sense of control. A temporary fix was better than ongoing pain.

Going through a divorce at age 27 upped the ante. I was entering the dating world for the first time in five years. The Dallas singles scene seemed to consist of Barbie dolls and G.I. Joes. Everyone seemed to be tanned, thin, muscular, gorgeous and fashionable. Plastic surgery and shopping seemed to be serious hobbies. I learned the rules pretty quickly — for the most part, they were the same ones that I had been following for years, only stricter: stay thin, be successful, have a perfect body, wear the right outfit. In short, improve, improve, improve!

I needed little outside pressure to send me into a new appearance frenzy. I exercised religiously and used fashion as a security blanket. I bought myself breast implants and briefly considered liposuction. I treated every extra calorie as if it were potentially lethal. During times of business or personal stress, I would suddenly lose control and "treat myself" to a pint of Haagen-Dazs or a drive-through dinner at Grandy's. Although I admitted it to no one, sometimes I used vomiting to get rid of the food and the guilt after these binges.

I don't remember the date, but I clearly remember the specific incident that triggered the end of my ongoing battle to improve my appearance. I was going out for the evening. Consistent with my *modus operandi* at the time, I had bought a trendy new outfit for the occasion. I had carefully applied my new makeup and had been relatively pleased with my reflection in the mirror.

And then I stepped into the elevator. A well-dressed, very attractive woman with thick blonde hair and blue eyes was on her way out. Between the fourth floor and the lobby, I saw my appearance in the elevator mirror deteriorate in front of my eyes. My hair suddenly looked thin and scraggly, and my outfit no longer felt good. I felt fat and was acutely aware of every less-than-perfectly toned body area. I felt myself becoming depressed, as a familiar voice inside my head negatively compared me to this stranger. I wanted to go back to my apartment and hide.

Suddenly I had a glimmer of the truth. It wasn't my body that was constantly changing, it was *my perception* of it. My face looked the same, with or without other people around. I was dieting, exercising and shopping, and yet I didn't look like the models I envied in the magazines. My arsenal of beauty strategies hadn't prevented the depression and insecurity that surfaced in the elevator. I finally began giving up the fantasy that I could improve myself into a better relationship with my appearance.

I realized that I could either work to obtain a healthier perspective of my appearance or I could continue to agonize over every perceived flaw. I could constantly try to conform to a relentlessly demanding cultural beauty ideal or I could become aware of these pressures and learn to handle them in a constructive way. I could improve my self-esteem or I could continue to use temporary fixes. I could develop a consistent, caring plan for myself or I could continue with my "drill-sergeant" mentality and erratic behavior. For the first time, I admitted that I was tired of my appearance obsession. I wanted to understand it and change it.

From my personal as well as my professional experience, I am well aware of the powerful influence the beauty standards have on us as individuals. I know that those are not going to go away overnight. Even today I continue to struggle with my own appearance periodically, particularly when my life is stressful.

However, I am more secure about my appearance than I ever thought possible. I am more aware of cultural influences, and therefore more in control of my response to them. I give them less power than I used to.

My perception of my body and my appearance no longer fluctuates with various circumstances. I know what situations and thoughts tend to trigger negative body feelings, and I have learned to modify my thoughts and adjust to a variety of situations. I have learned to improve my self-esteem in a variety of ways, not all of them related to my appearance.

I have gradually embraced a personally satisfying plan of exercise, nutrition and shopping. I have come to appreciate the stress-relieving aspects of exercise as much as the look-good aspects. I am more sensitive to the effects of various foods on my body, and make food selections based more on health than on calories. I still wear makeup, but I am less dependent on it to feel like I look okay. I still love to shop, yet I have learned to recognize signs that I am overusing fashion to relieve stress and try to find some temporary boost that I can give myself in a nonfinancial way! I am more content than I have ever been.

How did my personal experience influence my work as a clinical psychologist? How did my clinical expertise fit into my personal struggles? Right out of graduate school I worked with teenagers and young adults. As a young practitioner, I could relate well to these age groups. I saw clients who were depressed, had been sexually abused, were getting out of painful relationships, were having trouble with their parents. I saw kids who were struggling with grades, worrying about popularity and experimenting with drugs. And I began to see more and more females with eating disorders.

I have specialized in eating disorders since I opened my private practice. I see outwardly beautiful models who are struggling with appearance issues (and have learned that not even models look like magazine covers without three hours of makeup!). Alongside these unhappy and appearance-obsessed models, I see overweight women who are convinced that their lives would be complete if they had a different body shape or were more attractive. When speaking to various groups on eating disorders and the impact of our society's emphasis on physical appearance, I am often struck by how attractive are the many people I encounter who have painful relationships with their appearance.

Even with my own past concerns with weight, I am amazed at the harmful lengths some of my therapy clients go to in order to either "improve" their bodies or prevent deterioration. Hearing one client describe her ten-year pattern of vomiting six times a day, or another tell of her three-hour-a-day exercise routine, is horrifying.

Yet hearing a close friend relate her mother's sixth bout with plastic surgery inspires similar feelings. At parties, conversations about diet and exercise invoke immediate flashbacks of recent therapy sessions. Women compare diet tips and men compete with bodybuilding talk. Men shop for hair replacement and women scout for men with hair. The longer I research our culture's attitude toward beauty, the stronger my belief that we are all insecure about our appearance and our bodies. We are all trying to match unrealistic standards that are set by media and advertisements. My eating disorder clients use extreme methods, but they seem to be seeking the same goals as the majority of young to middle-aged Americans — and they are equally unsuccessful.

Inventing a balanced way to cope with our society's obsession with physical beauty has been my motivating task over the past four years. I've read hundreds of articles. I've talked extensively to friends, people in the modeling business and other individuals. I've conducted surveys and developed workable techniques with my clients. Most challenging, I have worked hard on my own appearance obsession. In this book I'd like to share with you what I've learned on my path from appearance obsession to appearance security.

ARE YOU
APPEARANCE
OBSESSED?

When I think about my appearance in comparison to the women in magazines and on TV, I feel insecure and have low self-esteem. Then I get angry at myself for feeling insecure and having low self-esteem.

Female accountant, age 39

Our society's emphasis on physical appearance makes me feel like I must be competitive in my looks and go to certain lengths to compete with others. It frustrates me that most people are interested in looks first, personality second. It frustrates me more that I am that way, and I blame our society along with myself.

Male stockbroker, age 24

Appearance Obsession: A Cultural Phenomenon

It's a fact that physical attractiveness is prized in our culture. There is nothing wrong with wanting to "look good." When we feel good about the way we look, the appearance messages in our society can work in our favor. For example, in my personal research, some survey respondents noted that our society's emphasis on looks motivated them to take care of themselves through a healthy diet and regular exercise.

Unfortunately, this was a very small minority. Even those who responded in this way often wrote about the negative motivation that frequently triggered their caretaking behavior, that is, the fear of losing their body shape, of gaining weight, of losing muscle bulk, and so on. Appearance pressures in our society can easily turn into a chronic dissatisfaction with our appearance and a never-ending pursuit of self-improvement.

In Chapter 1, I shared with you my personal struggle with appearance obsession. Over the past four years, I have talked with, counseled and surveyed hundreds of men and women of all shapes, sizes and looks, and I have discovered:

- Very few of us are satisfied with our looks.
- A person's outward appearance has little relationship to his or her self-esteem or sense of personal attractiveness.
- The majority of us feel trapped and confused about the role of physical appearance in our lives. We like looking good, yet don't feel that we measure up. We like being thin but are never thin enough.
- Self-improvement is not enough.

As you can see, a cultural problem has created a lot of personal pain. This book will help you assess the degree to which our society's obsession with looks is hurting you so that you can get some perspective on the role of looks in your life.

As you will see, the answer to coping with our society's obsession with looks isn't to criticize or dictate personal choices, but to expand your avenues for feeling good about yourself. Rather than limiting your self-improvement options, this book will help you realistically assess the benefits and drawbacks of self-improvement and offer healthy guidelines for eating, exercise and shopping. Rather than set new "improved" beauty guidelines, you will learn to aim for a balance between self-improvement and self-acceptance, a balance that is based on your personal desires and goals rather than culturally dictated prescriptions.

What's Happening To Us?

Swimsuit sections in women's magazines seduce us with pictures of the "perfect body." "Before" and "after" diet pictures speak not only to the physical changes of weight loss, but strongly suggest a drastic lifestyle improvement. "Have more dates, more excitement, more business success, more everything with less weight!" *Muscle and Fitness* magazine offers tips for men on body-sculpting and gives "how-to" advice for men seeking that ever-illusive "chiseled stomach." Hair-replacement commercials sell self-confidence along with their products, again reinforcing the need to "look good to feel good."

The American preoccupation with physical appearance has provided us with impossible rules and guidelines about how we are supposed to look, and we are desperately trying to measure up: 80 percent of American women have dieted by age 18. Eleven percent of high school seniors have eating disorders. The number of people seeking plastic surgery has escalated in the last ten years; between 1981 and 1990, liposuction procedures mushroomed 95 percent and, in spite of the recent controversy, breast implants actually increased in popularity from 1988 to 1990. Steroid use to build strength has skyrocketed, and up to one-third of all plastic surgery candidates are men (compared to 6 percent ten years ago).

In addition to the barrage of dieting, exercise and plastic surgery options, cultural beauty values have taught us to pursue self-improvement over self-acceptance. We have learned to judge our inside by our outside, and to strive for unattainable physical perfection. For many men and women, this emphasis has resulted in an often destructive appearance obsession (see Figure 2.1.).

Aren't Beauty Standards Normal?

Every society throughout history has provided physical appearance guidelines for men and women, particularly women. Never before, however, has the price of participation in a culture's beauty pageant been so high. For the first time, the availability and diversity of the media is phenomenal, as is the media's influence on our perception of the world. Consider the following:

Figure 2.1.
Cultural Appearance Obsession

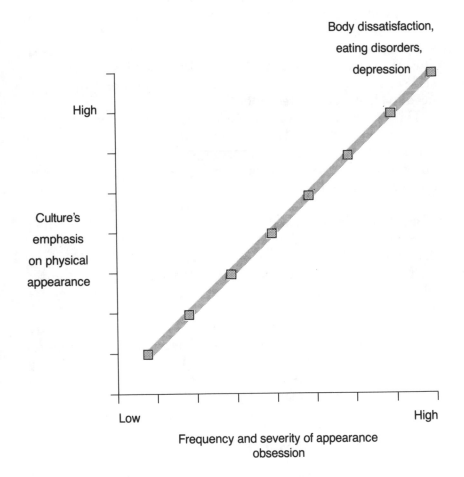

1. Weight concerns and dissatisfaction with body shape are so common among women today that a 1985 symposium attempted to define the "normal level of discontent" that American women feel toward their appearances.

2. Body image is more closely linked to self-image in America than in any other culture. While Japanese teenagers actually rate their body satisfaction lower than their American counterparts, their self-image and self-esteem are significantly higher.

3. In *every* culture that has the "thin is in" beauty ideal, there is a dramatic increase in depression and eating disorders among women beginning in adolescence. This is true *only* in cultures that have this beauty ideal.

Assessing The Impact On Ourselves

Our culture's appearance obsession affects almost everyone. However, the degree that it affects us, and the ways we cope with it, vary from individual to individual. Use the following questionnaire to see where you fall on the appearance obsession continuum.

Appearance Obsession Questionnaire

Put a check beside the statements that are true for you. Use the scoring system at the end of the questionnaire to see how you are doing in comparison to other American men and women. Write down the numbers of the questions you endorsed; we will use these later in the chapter.

1. ____ I exercise at least three times a week.

2. ____ I feel anxious if I miss one workout.

3. ____ I find myself putting off decisions until I "lose weight" or "get in shape."

4. ____ I diet at least one week out of every month.

5. ____ I weigh myself at least once a day.

6. ____ I feel a lot of pressure to look good.

7. ____ Buying new clothes is a major way I relieve stress.

8. ____ I frequently compare my looks to others.

9. ____ I use fashionable clothes to compensate for the negative view I have of my body.

10. ____ I have avoided social situations because I didn't have the right outfit.

11. ____ The way I appear to others is frequently not the way I am really feeling.

12. ____ I do not go out in public without making sure I look good.

13. ____ I would like to lose weight.

14. ____ I feel threatened by attractive persons of the same sex.

15. ____ I find myself acting dramatically different depending on the situation and the people I am with.

16. ____ I think our society places too much emphasis on looking good.

17. ____ I think my life would improve if my face or body was different.

18. ____ I am very sensitive to comments about my looks.

19. ____ I am easily influenced by fashion advertisements.

20. ____ I believe that a person is totally in control of his/her weight.

21. ____ My perception of the way I look depends on the mood I'm in.

22. ____ People exercise primarily to look better.

23. ____ I have had cosmetic surgery.

24. ____ I often feel trapped in a certain role.

25. ____ I binge (eat well past the point of fullness) at least once a week.

Scoring: For each question you checked, give yourself one point. Total your points, and read on to see what your score suggests.

0-5: You are coping with our society's obsession with looks fairly well. As we saw earlier in the chapter, most American women, in particular, are dissatisfied with their appearance and cope through some combination of dieting, shopping or exercise. In short, you are in good company!

It may be helpful to take this questionnaire two steps further. First, regardless of how you scored in comparison to others, the important factor is how *you* feel about your score. If you are unhappy with your appearance, or spend more energy than you want to on appearance-related tasks, this book is for you. Second, at the end of this chapter you will assess your pattern of responses. This will help you identify any patterns or problem areas that deserve attention.

6-10: Your score suggests that our society's looks obsession may be affecting how you feel about yourself and what you do. You are likely to be sensitive to appearance pressures, and may feel confined by a need to monitor your behavior and your appearance closely. It will be important to assess your pattern of responses to see specifically how your appearance obsession is influencing your life.

10 or more: Your responses indicate that you are preoccupied and dissatisfied with your appearance. Internal appearance pressures may sometimes control your behavior, and you may feel trapped in a never-ending cycle of self-improvement. You are likely to be very sensitive to appearance aspects of your environment, and may feel easily influenced by media messages that promote dieting, shopping or fashion. Assess your pattern of answers at the end of this chapter to identify particularly vulnerable areas.

What Is Appearance Obsession?

Appearance obsession is a chronic, painful preoccupation with physical appearance. To a large extent, it is a normal attempt to cope with our society's glorification and endless pursuit of physical perfection. However, what's normal isn't necessarily what is healthy. We who are appearance obsessed have certain patterns of thinking, feeling and behaving in relation to our appearance, and almost all of these result in an ongoing sense of failure and inadequacy.

Here are some of the symptons of appearance obsession:

Thoughts:

- Frequently compare looks to others: "Look at her stomach. I wish mine was flat like that."
- Drill sergeant self-talk (motivate yourself out of fear): "You *are* going to aerobics, I don't care if you're tired. How do you think you'll feel if you get flabby?"
- Self-critical (think negative thoughts when you look in the mirror): "I look so fat. Look at those thunder thighs. Why are my eyes so close together? I look like an owl."
- Self-conscious (constantly monitoring how we appear to others): "I hope he likes my outfit. I wonder if she's looking at that good-looking guy in the corner? I shouldn't have said that, now he'll think I'm stupid."
- Self-berating ("beat self up" mentally): "Great! You've blown your diet again. Can't you stick with anything?"

Feelings:

- frustration
- depression
- embarrassment
- shame
- helplessness
- insecurity
- mood swings

Behaviors:

- chronic dieting
- excessive exercise
- excessive shopping
- appearance checking
- constant self-improvement
- plastic surgery
- weighing self once a day or more
- avoidance of social events that emphasize looks or bodies

When we are appearance obsessed, we constantly diet, exercise compulsively and rely on fashion to soothe, temporarily, the perpetual dissatisfaction we feel about our bodies and our looks. We carry around an ongoing sense of frustration and helplessness because we inevitably fail to meet the ideal beauty standards. We rely on looking good for approval and a temporary sense of security. We endlessly monitor what we present to others out of fear that they will pick up on our appearance insecurities. What would we do if others saw us as we really see ourselves?

Appearance obsession occurs *regardless* of the actual size, weight or level of one's objective physical attractiveness. I see models who painfully obsess about every perceived flaw, and medically overweight women who fantasize about a different life if "only I could lose weight." I see men who receive a tremendous amount of attention for their looks, yet constantly look for a new person to reaffirm that they *really are* handsome enough. Appearance obsession has to do with *how we see ourselves*, not with how others see us.

As appearance-obsessed individuals, we create a vicious circle for ourselves whereby we set high goals and then battle and push ourselves to meet these goals. One of two things happens: we fail to meet these perfectionistic goals and berate ourselves for our lack of willpower and after a period of self-recrimination, we start again. Or, if we meet our initial goal, we may allow ourselves a brief period of satisfaction, but soon we are setting higher and harder goals for ourselves. The five characteristics of appearance obsession help explain how and why this vicious circle is created.

Characteristics Of Appearance Obsession

The characteristics of appearance obsession may sound familiar to you: are you overly concerned with self improvement? Are you always dissatisfied with some part of your body? Does your concept of how you look change depending on who you're with? Let's take a closer look at these, and more.

IMPROVEMENT ORIENTED

Anne is a 23-year-old college graduate. She has worked part-time as a model since age 13, and uses this money in part to pay for her college education. She is bright, attractive and painfully obsessed with her appearance.

"I exercise seven days a week and am constantly on a diet. I spend about a third of my monthly income on clothes, and have gotten into financial trouble due to my shopping sprees. It is almost impossible for me to go to a new store without buying a new outfit. I constantly feel insecure about my looks — it gets worse when I am around other models.

"My friends tease me about the numerous diet articles and magazines I've read — sometimes I laugh with them, but sometimes it embarrasses me. No one wants to listen to me complain about my looks. After all, I am a *model*.

"I just wish I could see myself the way others do. Every time I look in the mirror, I find myself focusing on the parts of my looks that I don't like. I keep thinking, 'If I just get rid of that trouble spot there, or if I just lose weight, then I'll be happy with myself.' So far it hasn't worked, but at least I feel better about myself while I'm trying to look better."

A powerful part of appearance obsession is the seduction of looks improvement. Not everyone goes to the same extent that

Anne does to try to improve her appearance. Sandy goes on a diet one week, "blows it" the next week and then starts again. She hasn't lost weight and she frequently criticizes herself for her lack of willpower, yet she is determined to stick with this pattern until she is "successful."

John bodybuilds five times a week and has taken steroids on several occasions. Bob, on the other hand, will start an exercise program, increase it to the point that it becomes unbearable and then quit. He is competing so much with himself, with his internal ideal body, that what starts out as fun becomes a chore and a self-defeating activity.

When we are appearance obssessed, we are constantly trying to improve ourselves through keeping up with the latest fashion, dieting, exercising five times a week or buying a different brand of makeup. We are in a constant state of anxiety about food. We become anxious if we miss one workout, fantasizing that this is just the beginning of a downslide into lethargy and thunder thighs.

We motivate ourselves out of fear and social pressure. We confuse self-acceptance with laziness and a lack of discipline. We carry around an underlying sense of inadequacy about our looks, coupled with a strong sense of duty to improve them.

Take Another Look

First, make a list of self-improvements that includes every appearance-related activity you undertake each week. Include activities such as hair appointments, getting ready in the morning, reading diet books or fashion magazines, your regular exercise schedule, the amount of time you spend shopping each week. To qualify for the list, the activity should be related to your appearance and the goal should be to "look better."

Next, make a list of self-nurturing activities — taking a bubble bath, reading a good book, socializing with a close friend, engaging in a fun physical activity. The activity should be related to relaxation and the goal should be pleasure. Activities on this list should not feel like they require work!

Compare and contrast these two lists. Are they equal in length? If your self-improvement list is much longer, and particularly if you do not have at least two self-nurturing activities consistently scheduled each week, begin to expand your self-nurturing activities. The goal is to get a balance that feels good to you.

NEGATIVE BODY IMAGE

Sara: *You have such a good body. I wish I had legs like you do. I exercise and exercise and I can never get rid of the cellulite on the back of my thighs.*

Cynthia: *You can't be serious. I hate my body. I wish my stomach was flat. I always notice women with flat stomachs. I've always wanted to be as tall as you — and your self-discipline about exercise makes me sick.*

How many times have you heard a conversation like this one in the locker room of a health club? Maybe you've had a similar conversation yourself.

A second characteristic of appearance obsession is a chronically negative body image. Simply put, it means that no matter how our body looks to others, we don't think it looks good enough. We don't like the way it looks to us. We focus on those "less than perfect" parts, and minimize or ignore the ones we do like. After all, they aren't the source of our anguish. We overestimate our body size. And like Cynthia, we particularly notice other people who have body parts that we would like to have.

Cynthia focuses on stomachs because she is unhappy with hers. Sara notices legs because she feels deficient in the legs department. As a result, they evaluate themselves and others by different criteria. The outcome, however, is the same: Cynthia and Sara pick out ideal stomachs and legs, and feel depressed and insecure when they encounter them.

A negative body image affects us in many different ways. Research indicates that body image has a lot more to do with perceptions than it does with reality. It is what we think of our bodies rather than how they actually look that is the key. Remember Anne? Objectively she has met most of the criteria for our "ideal" appearance; after all, she's a model. Yet Anne is continually dissatisfied with her appearance and has a painful relationship with her bedroom mirror.

Most of us know if we have a negative body image. We feel dissatisfied when we look in the mirror. We diet in an attempt to shrink our bodies; we lift weights in an attempt to expand or mold them. We compare our bodies to others and lose the competition. We may have had plastic surgery, yet we continue to focus unhappily on areas of concern. In short, we don't like what we see.

Take Another Look

When you think of your body, on what parts do you focus? With what parts are you satisfied? In Chapter 10, we will assess our degree of satisfaction with a number of body parts. For now, begin focusing on those parts of your body with which you *are* satisfied. No one is unhappy with *every* aspect of their appearance. What parts can you begin to appreciate?

FRAGILE APPEARANCE ESTEEM

In Chapter 1, I shared with you the abrupt change in my appearance satisfaction as a result of my chance encounter with a woman in an elevator. That story reflects the third component of appearance obsession — fragile appearance esteem.

Fragile appearance esteem means that the way we feel about our appearance is vulnerable to outside and inside influences. If we feel depressed over a fight with our boyfriend, we look in the mirror and think we're ugly. We boost our appearance esteem with an aerobics class, but it crashes with the next broken diet. We feel slightly better about our workout if the person next to us has a "worse" figure, but it's bad news if the person standing next to us has a "better" body.

Fragile appearance esteem leads us to be sensitive to remarks about our appearance. We feel threatened by attractive members of our own sex, especially if we don't know them. We are easily influenced by advertisements because their promises of glamour and excitement through fashion appeal to our constant search for appearance security.

Take Another Look

Begin thinking about events or people that affect the way you feel about your looks. What compliments are especially meaningful to you? What are some ways that you can give those compliments to yourself?

SELF-CONSCIOUS RELATIONSHIPS

I find myself pulling for reassurance from others about how I look. My boyfriend says I drive him crazy asking him how I look in a certain outfit, if he thinks I'm gaining weight and so on. I know that I do — I just can't seem to help myself sometimes. Then I get afraid that he'll start seeing me the way that I do.

Female model, age 19

When I go out with a new woman, I find myself constantly monitoring what I say, my gestures, how I look and so on. It's like there's a part of me in the background, constantly evaluating my performance. You know those judges at a gymnastics competition? There is a part of me holding up a card with a number on it, saying you're doing okay or you're blowing it.

Male real estate agent, age 33

I hate to admit it, but there's an immediate barrier when I meet a beautiful woman for the first time. I feel jealous and threatened by her. I feel so insecure about my own appearance that being around someone that I think is incredibly attractive just makes it worse.

Female student, age 29

Each of these statements describes how appearance obsession can affect our relationships. We feel fragile about our own looks, so we evaluate other people's looks, bodies and clothes — and are sure that they are doing the same! We never go out in public without making sure we look as good as possible. No matter how we feel, we put only our best face forward.

We may have a hard time establishing a friendship with an attractive member of our own sex; we do enough mental comparing without having a friend as an attractive reminder that we are not measuring up to our "ideal." We compete with members of the same sex and have trouble sharing our insecurities and fears. Or we bond through our appearance obsession and spend a lot of time commiserating about our failed diets, flabby bodies and overspending. We pull boyfriends, girlfriends, best friends and spouses into our appearance obsession. If they just tell us *one more time* that we look okay, then maybe it will sink in!

No matter what form it takes, appearance obsession inter-feres with our ability and willingness to be intimate with others. In our interactions, we focus on how we are *appearing* to be, not how we are. We say what we think is the right thing and we try to wear the right outfit. We even avoid situations where we don't think this is possible. I have heard several people talk about missing a fun party because they didn't think they had the right thing to wear.

Take Another Look

How do your feelings about your appearance affect your rela-tionships? How easy is it for you to develop friendships with members of your sex? The opposite sex?

IMAGE EMPOWERMENT

I feel that all people should be happy with the way they look and that means looking good . . . I equate looks with happiness.

Female attorney, age 27

According to *Webster's New Collegiate Dictionary*, the word "em-power" means to "give official authority to." Those of us who are appearance obsessed empower our outward image and give it priority over all other aspects of ourselves. We try to ignore our feelings and concentrate on our appearance; in fact, when we are aware of our feelings, they are frequently negative and related to our looks. We judge our inside by our outside.

We tend to think if we look good enough, we will also feel good. Our self-esteem comes to mean our appearance esteem. When we concentrate on our looks and ignore our inner self long enough, however, we begin to feel like paper dolls — all dressed up but flat underneath.

When we are empowering our image, we are treating our ap-pearance the way we should treat ourselves. We sacrifice comfort for fashion. We ignore anxiety and stress about finances to have a new outfit for the next social occasion. We don't have time for a bubble bath or a meditation class because we can't see the benefits. We place our appearance at the top of our goals and squash any hint of rebellion.

Christi is a 25-year-old account representative with a busy work schedule and an active social life. She runs religiously and organizes her meals around her schedule. She always seems to know what clubs are "in" and what's in fashion. She subscribes to several fitness magazines as well as to *Cosmopolitan, Vogue* and *Glamour.* She is admired by many of her friends as someone who "always has it together."

Christi came to see me because she was tired of her dissatisfaction with her body and her looks. Even though other people thought she was attractive, Christi's appearance esteem continued to fluctuate with her mood, whether she had exercised or not, and many other variables. While her peers saw her as poised and confident, she felt insecure and inadequate beneath her fashionable outfit.

Christi realized that her constant attempts to improve her appearance were not helping her low self-esteem or her lack of confidence. She was in a constant state of fatigue due to her lifestyle, yet she was afraid to give it up. Like many of us, she had a lot of mixed feelings about her relationship with appearance.

"I get tired of constantly monitoring my appearance, but I get a lot of attention when I look good. If I get a better balance and focus on parts of myself that others can't see, maybe I'll feel worse because I won't have as many dates. If I quit pushing myself so hard, maybe I won't do *anything* to take care of my appearance. Maybe I'll get fat or flabby."

Take Another Look

How do you empower your image? What fears do you have about accepting your appearance? Are you afraid that you'll have fewer dates, lose control of your eating or quit exercising? List every fear that comes to mind on a sheet of paper. How realistic are they?

How To Overcome Appearance Obsession

Appearance obsession is a distinct syndrome with identifiable characteristics and symptoms, yet throughout this chapter we heard differing examples of the various ways appearance obsession disrupts our lives. Some of us focus on our weight; we diet

repeatedly, weigh ourselves at least once a day and let the bathroom scale dictate our mood for the day. Some of us exercise to
the point of fatigue, yet continue to focus on that one trouble
spot that never seems to go away. All of us are dissatisfied with
our appearance and constantly seek to improve it. If we can't
improve ourselves into a better relationship with our appearance,
what can we do?

When we become aware of our culture's beauty ideals and the
way they bombard us through the media, we can begin to evaluate
them more objectively. We can then assess the ways that our
culture's beauty standards are influencing us, and begin to acknowledge the chronic pain and dissatisfaction we feel about our
appearance and the treadmill we are running on in an attempt to
improve our looks. We can identify specific behaviors, thoughts
and feelings that characterize our own special brand of appearance obsession and gradually move toward a balance between an
outer focus and an inner focus. Ultimately, we can achieve a
peaceful compromise between self-improvement and self-acceptance (see Figure 2.2.).

Figure 2.2. Getting A Balance

Self-Improvement   Self-Acceptance
Outward Focus   Inward Focus

Exercise: Appearance-Obsession Clusters

To begin this process, look at the questions you endorsed on the appearance obsession questionnaire. Earlier in the chapter, you were able to score yourself and place yourself in an appearance-obsession category. We are now going to do a cluster analysis so that you can begin to identify the specific ways that your appearance- obsession is affecting you.

Compare the item numbers on your list to the appearance-obsession clusters listed below. Which clusters do most of your answers fall into? Are you having the most trouble with relationships? With dieting or shopping? Rank the clusters in the order in which you endorsed the most items. Use this ranking to assist you as you go through the rest of this book.

Appearance-Obsession Clusters:

- Exercise: 1, 2, 3, 6, 16, 17, 22
- Shopping: 6, 7, 9, 16, 19
- Dieting: 3, 4, 5, 6, 13, 16, 20, 25
- Relationships: 6, 8, 10, 11, 12, 14, 15, 16, 18, 24
- Body Image: 6, 16, 17, 21, 23

I encourage you to read Chapters 3 and 4 next. After that, however, you may want to begin with the chapter that deals specifically with the cluster that is the most problematic for you. In that chapter you will find specific exercises and information that will help you with that particular aspect of appearance obsession.

A Final Note: Are Men And Women Different?

Many women in the groups I speak to react with surprise when I say that appearance obsession is also a problem for men. Both men and women seem to perceive beauty standards as a women-only trap, and historically this is certainly true. It is only in the past ten years that men have begun to struggle with some of the same appearance pressures that women have felt throughout time, and in comparison to women their share of the burden continues to be less.

However, without question, men are competing with their appearance. Because of a different beauty ideal, the ways that appearance obsession manifests itself in men tends to be somewhat different.

In comparison to women, men are more likely to:

- use steroids
- bodybuild
- excessively compete with peers
- overcompensate for their appearance insecurity through outward arrogance and overconfidence

They are *less* likely to:

- diet
- get facial plastic surgery

Turn to Chapter 3 to find out why.

THE BEAUTY
CULTURE CLUB

Thousands of young girls in schools, colleges and offices are not dieting, as they fondly believe, but are starving themselves . . . the modern girl . . . is so afraid of being overweight that she is not willing to be of even normal weight.

New York Times, October 12, 1926

Reading the above quote may initially lead us to believe that thin has always been in. For those of us who grew up in the sixties, seventies and eighties, it may be hard to believe that there has ever been a beauty standard for women that didn't include "thin." Yet in reality the beauty standard for women has fluctuated dramatically over time and within various cultures.

There's No Such Thing As A "Natural Beauty"

In twentieth century America, every decade has had its own standard of feminine beauty. If we had grown up as large-breasted women during the flapper era of the 1920s, for example, fashion would dictate that we bind our chests in order to wear the latest style. When larger figures became popular in the 1930s, we might have gorged on food in an attempt to meet the voluptuous ideal body. And as fifteenth century European women, we would have strived for still another look. Following the bubonic plague and the resulting population depletion, the standard of beauty was the *pregnant* look. Women would go to great lengths to achieve this, primarily by wearing a full gown with pillows or other forms of stuffing underneath.

Clearly politics and economics play a large part in setting beauty standards for women. It wasn't by accident, for instance, that the fifteenth century pregnant beauty ideal bloomed at a time when the European population was low. Worldwide, cultures with a high rate of poverty and malnutrition tend to idealize full figures in an environment where thin equals poor and fat symbolizes wealth and prestige.

These political and economic factors and the resultant beauty standards are completely out of our personal control, yet they can exert a lot of control over us. As many of us know firsthand, they can have devastating effects on our personal view of ourselves.

If we could go back and visit other cultures and periods throughout history, some of the beauty trends would seem somewhat bizarre. Yet the individuals living during those times undoubtedly viewed those beauty standards as normal. We learn the ideal beauty standards of our culture at an early age, and because we often don't have a basis of comparison we come to accept them as reality.

Some women — by the luck of the draw — meet the prevailing beauty standards and are called "natural" beauties. But it's important to remember that because beauty ideals are learned, and vary across culture and time, there is really no such thing as a "natural" beauty. Given the right time period and the right culture, all of us could enjoy a place on the pedestal of a culture's beauty ideal. Unfortunately, few of us (if any) can live up to the unprecedented beauty ideals of twentieth century America. For women, these unrealistic ideals begin with "thin."

THE HISTORY OF THIN-IS-IN (AGAIN)

The thin-is-in beauty ideal for American women emerged in

the 1920s, went underground during the 1940s and 1950s, came back into favor with Twiggy in the 1960s and has dominated ever since. There are many theories behind its popularity. One interesting finding is that the thin beauty ideal emerges during periods when women have broken new frontiers in terms of equal rights. Men and women tend to link a rounder figure and larger breasts with femininity. As women take on new roles that traditionally have been held by men, the thin look may symbolize a rejection of femininity and an emphasis on a more masculine look.

Another popular notion is that societies with an abundance of food may come to view the ability to abstain from indulgence as a sign of internal strength and self-control. Just as societies with a high poverty rate tend to view plumpness as a sign of wealth and prestige (and beauty), Western cultures tend to view thinness as a symbol of success.

As culture has become increasingly complex, so have beauty standards. The past 30 years have brought us an increasingly difficult beauty ideal. While the 1960s reintroduced the thin beauty ideal, during the 1970s and 1980s we got additional beauty criteria — fitness and muscle tone. For most women the beauty standards of the nineties have become so complex as to be absurd.

As women struggle to do it all by combining traditional passive and domestic female roles with those assertive and powerful career options, we are also told to "just do it" and obtain a perfect body ideal. The "new" beauty standard reflects these expanded and often confusing roles. The nineties beauty standard, called the "hybrid," consists of shapely (but not too muscular) arms, large breasts, a flat stomach, small hips and long, muscular legs. As we struggle to achieve a balance between the traditional female tasks of home and child care, and the newly available career tasks, we are also struggling to achieve a body balance. Thus today's "ideal woman" must have a feminine upper body with a svelte, almost masculine lower body. Do you know anyone who naturally possesses this body shape?

As American women, we get a double whammy: (1) we face an impossible beauty ideal, and (2) the emphasis on looks in American culture is unprecedented. Not only does our society dictate the beauty standards, it also tells us how important these beauty standards are to our overall self-concept. Our society's emphasis on beauty dramatically influences our overall sense of self in comparison to other cultures. As we saw in Chapter 2, Japanese teenagers give a lower satisfaction score when evaluating their bodies, yet their overall self-concept is higher than their American counterparts. For twentieth century American teenagers, particularly adolescent girls, body image is so crucial that we can virtually predict a girl's self-image by exploring her body image.

THE POLITICS OF FACE

Plastic surgery was the fastest-growing medical specialty of the 1980s. When faces go in and out of style, why wouldn't it be? Because the "face of the eighties" included fuller lips, collagen lip injections blossomed. Because women wanted to project an air of competence and confidence, this translated, in plastic surgery terms, into prominent cheekbones, wider eyebrows and deep-set eyes.

We are already seeing a new face of the nineties: thin eyebrows are back in style. Sure, we can all pluck our eyebrows now; but we can be certain that next year bushy brows will be peering at us from magazine covers. What do we do then?

I remember looking at Cybill Shepherd after she won the Model of the Year contest in the 1970s. I closely observed her blonde hair (which I didn't have), her blue eyes (which I didn't have), her long, chiseled nose (which I didn't have) and her thin lips (which I didn't have). For a while in my teens, my reflection in the mirror seemed much uglier after reading that Eileen Ford let potential models know she would never accept a pug nose.

The beauty ideal of the nineties has also entrapped men who are seeking the "boardroom" look through plastic surgery. A "weak" chin is replaced with a "strong" one. Men concerned over the potential impact of wrinkles on their business success are getting facelifts to retain what they see as a vital and youthful presence. Success for men is coming to mean looking successful as well as being successful.

Like bodies, faces reflect the politics of the times. The increasing availability of methods to alter our looks, however, is relatively new. With this increasing availability has come an underlying pressure to keep up with the facial fashion. An increasing association of looks with personality characteristics or societal success puts added pressure on us to consider surgical remedies to even minor facial flaws or out-of-fashion features. But what do we do when the boardroom look is out and we still *have* the boardroom look?

Is The Media To Blame?

Society's beauty standards are strongly communicated to individual women. For example, 90 percent of all American girls ages 3 to 11 have a Barbie doll, an early role model with a figure that is *not attainable* in real life. And as early as 1972, the group Women on Words and Images found that popular primers inevitably included girl characters who were concerned about their looks. The boy characters never were.

Let's look at some other media messages for women:

1. In 1992, the ten popular magazines most commonly read by young men and women were reviewed for articles and advertisements related to weight loss. The result: the women's magazines contained 10.5 times more articles related to dieting and weight loss than did the men's magazines.
2. A study of the body measurements of *Playboy* magazine centerfolds and Miss America contestants for 1979 through 1988 found that the majority of women had a body weight 13 percent to 19 percent below the normal weight for women in that age group.
3. Sixty-nine percent of female television characters are thin, and only 5 percent are overweight.
4. Diet (for weight loss) and exercise articles in six popular women's magazines dramatically escalated between 1959 and 1988.
5. The average person sees between 400 and 600 advertisements *per day* — that is, 40 million to 50 million by the time he or she is 60 years old. One of every 11 commercials has a direct message about beauty.

And here's the impact on women:

1. Eight million Americans have an eating disorder.
2. Seventy percent of teenage girls diet.
3. Over 95 percent of all women overestimate their body size, often by as much as 25 percent.
4. A significant number of teenagers describe their "ideal girl" as being 5'7" tall, weighing 110 pounds and having blue eyes and long

blonde hair. Many of them also describe her in terms of her re-
semblance to Barbie.

5. Plastic surgery tripled between 1986 and 1988; 80 percent of the
surgeries were for cosmetic reasons.

The direct link between what we see and how we evaluate
ourselves is powerful. We see a distorted sample of super-thin
TV models, so we tend to overestimate our own body size. Girls
grow up idealizing Barbie, so they want to look like her. We are
encouraged (and taught how) to diet — and we do, even to the
point of developing an eating disorder.

THE ELASTIC BODY IMAGE

Looking at the latest swimsuit edition of *Sports Illustrated* is
likely to leave most women with a lingering sense of depression
and dissatisfaction. Short of smashing our TV or boycotting all
magazines, however, we are going to be exposed to media messages about the "right" way to look and advice on how to achieve
it. The media blitz of beauty messages is out of our control.

Nevertheless, the amount of exposure to society's beauty messages is something we can monitor. Research on the direct effects
of media advertising on our perception of our bodies and our
satisfaction with them provides a good argument that this may be
a worthwhile goal that has both long- and short-term payoffs.

In a 1992 study to assess the effect of television advertising and
programming on body image distortions, researchers Phillip Myers
and Frank Biocca exposed 76 female undergraduate students to
ideal-body media programming. They concluded that even 30 minutes of ideal-body commercials can negatively affect our perception
of our own bodies. Even short-term exposure to so-called ideal
bodies can result in a conflict between what we are seeing as ideal
and our own body perception, and cause us to exaggerate the size
of our own bodies. Imagine what happens over time!

Not only can media messages change the way we perceive our
bodies, they give us a false impression of what is normal. When
we see models that are five to six inches taller than the average
female, and 16 percent thinner, we develop unrealistic comparison standards. In fact, one of the medical criteria of anorexia
nervosa — a body weight 15 percent below that of the normal

population — would be met by the majority of models and beauty contestants.

The benefits of heavy makeup and special lighting aside, we begin to see women in a skewed fashion, made up of "beautiful" people who seem to achieve perfection effortlessly. No wonder our self-esteem suffers and we begin to engage in a variety of coping measures. Some studies have found a direct correlation between media consumption (the amount of time we spend reading fashion magazines and watching TV) and dieting and bulimic behaviors. The more appearance messages we see, the more pressure we feel and the more actively we try to cope.

ARE YOU OVEREXPOSED?

Do you:

- read at least three fashion magazines a month?
- watch at least two hours of TV a day?
- often find yourself talking about dieting and exercise?
- read every new diet or exercise book?
- frequently visit cosmetics counters?
- often compare yourself to magazine models?

If you answered yes to two or more of the above questions, you may be overexposing yourself to beauty messages. And as we have seen, overexposure often leads to appearance dissatisfaction and a self-improvement trap. At the end of this chapter, we will look at some specific strategies for taking personal control over the cultural beauty messages. For now, begin thinking about ways you can reduce your exposure to media beauty messages — and take some pressure off yourself!

Men And Physical Appearance

Men have traditionally been left out of the beauty standards spotlight because financial and career success are the traditional male benchmarks of prestige (and often self-worth). Even today, if we measure the impact of beauty standards on men through dieting and eating-disorder statistics, they are much further down the appearance-obsession ladder.

However, while women continue to report greater dissatisfaction with their appearance than men, new studies indicate that men may be closing the gap. Faced with more and more pictures of the ideal male body, as evidenced by the boom in bodybuilding magazines and body-sculpting articles, men are also beginning to experience a painful dissatisfaction with their bodies.

Consider a 1986 study conducted by *Psychology Today*. Only 18 percent of the male respondents stated that they were unconcerned about their appearance and did nothing to improve it. Men spent 2 billion dollars on hair-replacement products last year. In my own personal research of 306 men, men checked their appearances in the mirror as often as women and spent approximately the same amount as the female respondents each month on clothes. For the first time, men are also learning that the "mirror, mirror on the wall" telling them "who's the fairest of them all" is the media.

The Male Beauty Ideal: Why Now?

While women are struggling to balance new opportunities, today's men are scrambling to redefine their place at home and at work. With the blending and blurring of male and female roles, and the disappearance of traditional male frontiers, the body has become an increasingly important dimension by which men confirm their potency and identity. The soldier archetype embodied by the muscle-man look may be a way for men to demonstrate to others, and maintain for themselves, an ongoing sense of specialness and separateness as men in a society in which roles for men and women are increasingly blurred.

Given this soldier ideal, men are less likely as a group to engage in dieting and to develop eating disorders. Unlike women, for whom the adage "You can never be too thin" is still common, men are struggling against dual weight pressures. They don't want to be overweight or underweight. Underweight men are at increased risk for steroid abuse and compulsive bodybuilding. Overweight men are increasingly likely to diet; just like women, "fat" for men has come to symbolize lack of self-control, laziness and even femininity or softness.

MEDIA MESSAGES FOR MEN

Women aren't the only ones receiving media messages. Here are some aimed at men:

1. In comparison to women's magazines, men's magazines have a disproportionate number of articles that encourage change in body shape (through body-sculpting and weight training).
2. Advertisements and men's fashions have changed in style, both to accommodate and emphasize changes in men's physiques toward a more trim and muscular body. The newest window dummies are 6'2" tall, have 42-inch chests and need a size 42 suit. Compare these measurements to the old industry standard of a 38 regular.
3. Men are increasingly being targeted by diet programs. SlimFast, for example, recently featured a round of ads using well-known sports managers and celebrities (Tommy LaSorda, Joe Gibbs) as spokesmen for their weight-loss program.
4. Men spend approximately 2 million dollars a year on hair replacement formulas.

And here's the impact on men:

1. In surveys, between 70 and 80 percent of college males reported a discrepancy between their current body shape and their ideal. Most college males chose the extreme muscular build as their ideal, even though they saw themselves as average or even lean in terms of their current body structure.
2. Male clients constitute up to 30 percent of all plastic surgery candidates; ten years ago only 5 percent of all plastic surgery candidates were men. In addition, two new plastic surgery procedures designed specifically for men have emerged — pectoral and calf implants.
3. Steroid abuse continues to be a 300 million to 400 million dollar-a-year black-market business.
4. Twenty-five percent of all American men went on a diet in 1992.
5. Men have spent so much money on bogus products to stop balding that the government is considering taking action to get these products off the market.

Male And Female Appearance Pressures:
A Difference Of Degree

As part of my research for this book, I surveyed 768 men and women. Of the 461 women surveyed, 75 percent believe our society places too much emphasis on looks. Are you surprised to find that 70 percent of the 307 men agree? The difference between men and women was *the degree* to which they endorsed this statement. Sixty-two percent of the women strongly believe that our society places too much emphasis on looks, while 13 percent somewhat agreed. Fifty-four percent of the men agreed, or strongly agreed, with the overemphasis on beauty; an additional 16 percent endorsed this statement to a mild degree.

If we believe that our society places too much emphasis on looks, we are likely to be very conscious of and sensitive to our own appearance. Women who believed that our society is overly focused on looks also stated that they frequently compared their looks to others. These same survey respondents also described a high level of sensitivity to comments about their looks, and were likely to invest more time and energy getting ready each morning.

Men who were aware of our looks-conscious society were themselves looks-conscious. They reported a high degree of sensitivity about their own looks, and tended to devote more time to grooming in the morning. In fact, according to *Gentlemen's Quarterly*, the average amount of time today's man spends getting ready in the morning is 45 minutes, up from 30 minutes in the 1980s.

In response to the statement "I feel a lot of pressure to look good," 39 percent said definitely yes. Women endorsed this statement more often than men, a finding that is not surprising in light of our beauty heredity! Almost half of the women agreed (48 percent), while 26 percent of the men acknowledged similar pressure. Thus while a woman has a 50-50 chance of experiencing some degree of appearance obsession, slightly more than one of every four men is also struggling with these concerns.

In Chapter 2, we talked about the ambivalence many of us feel about our society's emphasis on looks. The results of this survey dramatically illustrate this. For women, agreement with the statement "I feel a lot of pressure to look good" virtually translates into "I don't like the way I look"; the more she agreed with this statement, the lower she rated her satisfaction with almost every body part. These findings suggest that the less satisfied a woman is with her overall appearance, the more pressure she feels; or the more pressure she feels, the less satisfied she is. Even a strong degree of dissatisfaction with one body area, such as abdomen or thighs, is associated with a sense of pressure about looks. While correlations don't tell us which comes first, the relationship between the two is evident.

So why doesn't she do something about it? You know, diet and work out, try to improve her looks? She does. Not only is the degree of appearance pressure, as indicated by a self-described pressure to "look good," associated with looks and body dissatisfaction, it is also associated with an increase in dieting and exercise. And perhaps in an attempt to prepare herself for a looks-conscious environment, she spends more time getting ready in the morning. The opposite relationship between appearance pressure and appearance satisfaction is just as strong for men.

We can draw some interesting hypotheses from this study. First, the majority of both men and women think that our society places too much emphasis on looks. Women are more likely than men to experience personal appearance pressures, yet men may be catching up. Finally, both men and women who are tuned into our society's emphasis on looks, and who feel pressure to live up to this emphasis, are more dissatisfied with their own appearance. They are also more likely to cope through some form of self-improvement. Our culture's focus on looks not only affects the way we feel about ourselves, it also influences our behavior.

Dispelling The Myths About Appearance

In Chapter 2, we saw the direct link between the cultural beauty ideals of thinness and the increased incidence of depression and eating disorders. In this chapter, we have explored direct messages we receive from the media about the ideal male and female body through a barrage of articles on diet, bodybuilding and exercise, and specific advice on how to achieve these ideals. We've also seen how exposure to these media messages directly influences what we do and how we feel about ourselves.

Beneath the overt beauty messages, however, are underlying communications about who and what we are as men and women. I call these our culture's beauty myths. It is these underlying assumptions and their implications that may eventually cause the most damage to our sense of satisfaction and self-esteem.

MYTH 1. OUR APPEARANCE IS UNDER OUR CONTROL

When we read advice on how to improve our looks, we get the underlying message that we have control over them. Whether it is finding the "right" diet to achieve a size six, or the perfect bodybuilding combination that will enable us to achieve that chiseled stomach, "how to" implies "you can." When we try these new, improved strategies, and they inevitably don't work, we also get the message "you didn't."

Throughout this book we will be talking about the role of genetics in determining body shape and appearance. I see 16-year-old boys with thin bodies, frantically lifting weights in an attempt to achieve a genetically unfeasible Arnold Schwarzenegger look. No matter how much they work out, they may never achieve their goal through exercise. If they succumb to using steroids to build bulk, they face health risks and long-term detrimental effects.

We all know someone who is a natural size ten but is permanently seeking a size six. Many diets later she's back to a size ten — her body the same size, her self-esteem a lot lower. Rather than question the advice we received, we question our self-control, our effort or our motivation. Maybe it is time to question the underlying (and never directly stated) assumption that is the basis of the advice: the assumption that we have direct control over our appearance.

MYTH 2. THE OUTSIDE REFLECTS THE INSIDE

Beauty messages not only encourage us to focus on our looks, they also teach us to make assumptions about each other based on physical appearance. They also warn us that if we aren't measuring up, others will make those same assumptions or judgments about us. Because of this, making assumptions based on looks is a double-edged sword. Not only are we likely to judge others based on outward appearance, we are also likely to believe that others are judging us. Whether they actually are or not, we may find ourselves feeling self-conscious in social situations or spend our energy wondering how we are doing on our date's beauty scale.

To some degree, we all compare ourselves with others to assess how we are doing. We compare grades in school, compete for work promotions and evaluate our achievements and financial successes. While we can certainly argue the pros and cons of the competitive focus of our society, at least in these areas we can attribute the outcome to effort, motivation or ability, factors that are under our control. When we compare appearance, however, we are truly on shaky ground.

Not only do we judge ourselves against others in the appearance category, we are also likely to attribute personality characteristics based solely on looks. For instance, thinness has not only come to represent attractiveness, it has also come to symbolize success, self-control and a higher socioeconomic class. We are all familiar with the extremely negative stereotypes associated with obesity (which appear to be equally strong for both men and women), but we may not be aware of more subtle attributes. Men also bear the brunt of the "outside is inside" myth; we tend to think that muscular, fit men have better social skills, more favorable personality traits and are more physically capable. This is in direct contrast to numerous studies that indicate body type has virtually no relationship to personality. How a person looks on the outside tells us *nothing* about the person on the inside.

MYTH 3. NORMAL IS WRONG

All of us get older, yet many of us come to fear the normal physical changes associated with aging. Women worry that their mate will leave them for a younger woman, and so they struggle to compete with nature. Men are beginning to link their appearance with job performance, and may worry that an aging face is interpreted as a sign of pending work deterioration. Rather than exploring the joys and benefits that come with each age, we are bombarded with warnings about the potential consequences of age. No wonder we head for the plastic surgeon at the first sign of wrinkles.

However, plastic surgery is no longer for the middle-aged. Body work is a choice for men and women of all ages, whether it is breast implants or "love-handles" removal. The problem lies not in an individual's choice but in the often painful motivation underneath. In fact, when we receive messages that our normal bodies are somehow inadequate, *not* taking steps to make them better somehow can feel like failure. The shame and secretiveness with which many people treat their history of plastic surgery, or their constant concern about their looks, clearly indicates that no matter what coping style one chooses, there are likely to be painful repercussions.

Personal Strategies For Our Beauty Culture

Men and women today face appearance pressures that are both complex and unobtainable. As individuals we have no direct control over cultural mandates, but we do have control over how much we expose ourselves to articles that encourage dieting, stringent fashion guidelines and overexercise. Let's look at some specific strategies for coping with our appearance-obsessed society.

STRATEGY 1. ASSESS YOUR MEDIA DIET

Pay attention to how much you expose yourself to appearance messages and assess how they affect you. For example, do you find yourself reading diet article after diet article, and then overeating in response to the depression that surfaces while you look enviously at the "after" pictures? Does your picture in the mirror look uglier after reading *Glamour* and *Vogue?*

If so, I strongly encourage you to reduce your media exposure, especially during the time you spend reading this book. Throw away the fashion magazines that are lying around your home or apartment. Broaden your reading; substitute a different kind of magazine or a favorite book as a replacement for a fashion magazine. Keep a daily journal and jot down your feelings and thoughts after you see or read beauty messages. Take down the "I want to look like her" picture on your refrigerator door and replace it with a happy memory.

Doing these exercises will help you focus on your feelings about yourself rather than send you into an automatic comparison with the latest fashion model or diet success.

STRATEGY 2. PUT YOUR APPEARANCE IN PERSPECTIVE

If you are a woman, you must understand that most of the

models you see in magazines would fit at least one of the criteria for anorexia nervosa. If you are a man, you must understand that if you take the bodybuilding magazines seriously, you may find yourself competing with a personal trainer — someone whose job requires hours working out at a gym. Getting our own perspective involves understanding that many of the messages we are currently getting are false and should be replaced with accurate information about dieting, exercise, shopping and realistic goals.

Putting your appearance in perspective means realizing that advertisments and magazines are slanted toward culturally attractive actors and actresses. It means understanding the relative nature of all beauty standards, and being able to step back and observe today's beauty messages without being controlled by them. Reading about beauty ideals in other cultures, or about the history of beauty in America, can be especially helpful in opening your eyes to the truly subjective nature of beauty.

Raising the accuracy level of your knowledge about looks, and focusing on factors over which you have direct control, can raise your commitment to conquering appearance obsession. For example, did you know that there is a normal 30-pound weight range for each sex, height and age? Do you know the risks of dieting, or the signs of overexercise? Most of us don't, and without a realistic basis for comparison we are more likely to rely on other sources, such as the media, for our information and our evaluation standard. When we do so, a painful consequence is likely.

STRATEGY 3. EXPLORE YOUR APPEARANCE CHOICES

What do you think would happen if you went without makeup one day a week? Give it a try one day a month. Challenging our routine responses to our society's focus on looks can be fun and informative. It can give us a new sense of freedom while providing us with valuable information about how we rely on our current ways of coping.

If you decide to explore your appearance choices, start small. Experiment with your clothes style; for instance, if you routinely wear closely fitting clothes, buy some that are loose and try wearing them. Spend less time getting ready for a social event and spend the leftover time relaxing and listening to your favorite music. The options are only limited by your imagination!

STRATEGY 4. EVALUTE YOUR ENVIRONMENT

When we endorse our society's beauty ideals, we tend to hang around other people who do. And, as you will see, we tend to be attracted to people who confirm what we already think of ourselves and the way we look. If we are critical of our looks, or are highly conscious of them, we are likely to be attracted to others who are also critical of our looks or who make frequent comments about them. This can obviously result in a never-ending cycle.

Dieters tend to hang around with friends who diet. Because most women diet I am certainly not advocating that you get rid of your dieting friends! What I am suggesting is that you should decide if dieting and looks need to be frequent topics of discussion. You may want to try getting out of the comparison trap or getting a better body image instead.

SETTING THE
STAGE: FAMILY
BEAUTY MESSAGES

Joy is a 17-year-old whose mother accompanied her to her first therapy session. Before coming to see me, she had told her mother that she was "a little depressed." Here's how Joy's mother described her during the initial interview:

"I just don't understand what is wrong. Joy is so beautiful — wherever we go, people are always commenting on how attractive she is. Look at that hair and those eyes; she certainly doesn't take after me. To be honest, I've often wondered how I got such a beautiful daughter. She has always looked like that."

Joy's mother then proceeded to describe Joy's popularity, her excellent grades and her numerous after-school activities. As her mother went on and on, Joy sank lower and lower in her chair, a gesture that was lost on her mother in her unceasing praise of her daughter. As the therapy sessions progressed, Joy told me that she was struggling with bulimia.

As we have seen, the conglomeration of beauty messages in our society puts us all at risk for appearance obsession. As individuals, however, we each have a unique beauty history. Some of our families were more concerned about looks than others. Growing up, we each received different feedback about our looks from friends and family members.

In this chapter, you will assess your personal beauty history. You will look at events or messages that may have put you at risk for appearance obsession, and then you'll identify how you can readjust a painful childhood body image. You will also explore ways you can handle the family beauty messages that you are currently receiving.

Girls At Risk

While all families tend to mirror cultural values to some degree, the extent to which these are communicated to boys and girls is different. When it comes to beauty messages, girls definitely get more than their share. In fact, research indicates that just being a girl loads the deck in favor of appearance obsession.

Girls are exposed to more direct messages about the importance of looks and, not surprisingly, these messages often result in a focus on appearance as we grow up. When we repeatedly receive these messages, it is natural and healthy to cope by doing things that we think will get us love and approval. Yet this can set us up by teaching us to focus on self-improvement rather than self-acceptance; to emphasize control and denial in relation to our bodies rather than respect and appreciation.

You can probably recall numerous comments about your childhood appearance. Adults tend to focus on the appearance of girls much more than on the appearance of boys. "Isn't she adorable," "What a beautiful dress" and "She looks just like a little doll" are compliments, yet they also send a clear signal that appearance and dress are important features of being a little girl. Parents who make a fuss about their daughter's beauty unwittingly communicate the importance of appearance early on, and this may come back to haunt them as their daughter reaches adolescence.

This is especially true when looks are the *major* source of attention. When talking about her childhood, Joy expressed considerable ambivalence about the role of looks in her life. On the one hand, she reported many happy memories as a child and noted that her looks had been a major source of "feeling good" for her as she had won several beauty contests.

At the same time, she felt trapped by the pressure she felt to be beautiful. In fact, Joy's jaunt into puberty precipitated her bulimia; as she had gained the normal body shape of an adult woman, she became increasingly frantic over the loss of her thin, prepubescent body and resorted to vomiting in an attempt to ward off additional weight gain. Even more important, the positive feedback of others was increasingly inconsistent with the dissatisfied view she now had of herself.

THE HURT CAN LINGER

If compliments can create a backlash, imagine what negative comments or teasing can do. Almost everyone I know can easily recall a hurtful nickname or a painful comment made by a peer, sibling or parent. "Chubby cheeks" or "bird legs" can result in embarrassment and self-consciousness; and when we hear them often enough, they can shape our adult perception of the way we look.

In my research, 31 percent of the women agreed or strongly agreed that they were teased about their appearance as a child. Furthermore, the women who reported childhood teasing were much more likely to be sensitive to comments about their appearance as adults, and to compare their looks to others.

These findings confirm what many of us already know: things we hear growing up have an impact on us as adults. Not only do they shape the way we view ourselves, they directly affect our adult behavior. The messages we hear as children create a special sensitivity in us that we spend a lot of time and energy trying to protect, fix or change as we get older. Every time we look in the mirror, we have a conversation with our reflection, comparing and contrasting what we see with what we remember.

While this is true for any characteristic, criticism about looks can leave an especially strong mark. This is because our own appraisal of our appearance, more so than many other personality characteristics, comes from what others say about us. In more objective areas, such as achievement or skills, no matter what messages we receive from others, we also get concrete feedback about how we are doing. We get grades in school or we successfully complete a project. Because looks are so subjective we have no objective basis of comparison.

In addition to the focus on appearance that little girls receive, the different ways that boys and girls are socialized may compound the problem. In her research on communication styles, Deborah Tannen describes the "connection" orientation that girls exhibit as early as ages three to four. A connection orientation simply means that girls are more likely to focus on relationships, and because of this focus they may rely more on interpersonal interactions as a major source of self-esteem. Thus, negative comments or criticism may have an especially detrimental impact on girls. Also, because our relationships, like our looks, are not completely under our control we may be more at risk for depression.

REASSESSING YOUR BODY IMAGE

Step 1: Make a list of all the comments you remember about your looks as a child.

Step 2: Evaluate this information. Were you warned about possible weight gain or teased about your small size? Did classmates call you "four-eyes" or ridicule your clothes? Did you get a lot of attention for "being pretty" or "being handsome"? At what age do your memories begin?

Who made the most comments — parents, siblings, peers, other adults? On the whole, were they positive or negative? Evaluating our memories gives us clues about the direction and focus of our early body image, how positive or negative it was and the people who had the most influence on its development.

Step 3: Now make a list of thoughts and feelings you have about your looks when you are standing in front of your mirror.

Step 4: Compare your list from Step 1 with your list from Step 3. Evaluate the similarities and the differences. What old messages are you continuing to give yourself? What messages are still hanging around but no longer fit?

After my somewhat "chubby" childhood, and messages about pending weight gain, it took me a while to realize the influence and power this lingering perception was continuing to have on my adult body shape. Separating painful memories from today's reality gives us the opportunity to begin creating a body image that is truly our own choice.

Assessing Your Family Risk Profile

Before we discuss family influence in the development of appearance obsession, answer the following questions. For each question circle the number that best describes your opinion:

1 = strongly disagree
2 = disagree
3 = somewhat disagree
4 = no opinion
5 = somewhat agree
6 = agree
7 = strongly agree

1. During my childhood and teen years, my mother was very weight conscious.

   1   2   3   4   5   6   7

2. I was considered attractive as a teenager.

   1   2   3   4   5   6   7

3. When I was a kid, I almost always immediately spent any money that I got.

   1   2   3   4   5   6   7

4. I was often teased about my appearance as a child.

   1   2   3   4   5   6   7

5. Looks were very important in my family.

   1   2   3   4   5   6   7

6. My father frequently made critical comments about my mother's appearance.

   1   2   3   4   5   6   7

7. I have a sibling who is more attractive than I am.

   1   2   3   4   5   6   7

8. "Having a boyfriend" was a priority that was communicated to me early on.

   1   2   3   4   5   6   7

9. My parents often pointed out "fattening" foods.

   1   2   3   4   5   6   7

10. For the girls in my family, shopping was a major leisure activity.

   1   2   3   4   5   6   7

11. My parents often attempted to control my eating/weight.

   1   2   3   4   5   6   7

12. I believe I was overweight as a child.

   1   2   3   4   5   6   7

13. I have a family history of an eating disorder.

   _____ True   _____ False

14. My family had very high expectations and goals for me.

   1   2   3   4   5   6   7

15. My mother was generally unhappy with her relationship with my father (or stepfather).

   1   2   3   4   5   6   7

16. The amount of money my mother spent on clothes was a source of conflict between my parents.

   1   2   3   4   5   6   7

17. One of my parents had plastic surgery.

   _____ True   _____ False

18. My mother was dissatisfied with her appearance.

   1   2   3   4   5   6   7

19. When I was a child, I could never save money long enough to buy something I really wanted.

   1   2   3   4   5   6   7

20. As a teenager, I often thought that my mother was less satisfied with the way I looked than I was.

   1   2   3   4   5   6   7

21. Compared to my friends' parents, my mother spent a lot of time on looks-related activities (shopping, beauty salon, dieting, exercise).

   1   2   3   4   5   6   7

22. For me to "look pretty" and "act like a girl" seemed important to my dad.

   1   2   3   4   5   6   7

23. My parents used to buy me just about everything I wanted.

1   2   3   4   5   6   7

Scoring: Add up the numbers that you circled for each question. For the True/False questions, give yourself five points if you answered True, one point if you answered False. Your total score should fall between 23 and 157.

90 or less: Your family risk factors were below average. You are likely to have a good foundation for coping with the cultural beauty messages.

91–105: Your family risk factors are in the average range. Write down the questions to which you answered 6 (agree) or 7 (strongly agree) to identify areas that were emphasized in your family. As you read the specific chapters that address each question, compare and contrast your current concerns and struggles with your answers to the family risk questions.

106 or higher: Your family risk factors are above average. A significant amount of energy was invested in physical appearance concerns, and your early role models may have communicated this to you. Write down the questions to which you answered 6 or 7 to identify areas that were emphasized in your family. As you read the chapters that address coping behaviors such as dieting, shopping and exercise, compare your current coping style with your family's past coping patterns. Pay close attention to the "Talking With Your Family Now" section below to see what you can do to prevent family beauty messages from affecting you today.

Like Mother, Like Daughter?

"Willpower" was Linda's immediate response when asked to describe the personality characteristic she most associated with her mother while growing up. Elaborating, she says, "My mother's control over her eating was incredible. She counted every calorie, exercised religiously and weighed herself every single day. She also controlled what we ate; we were not allowed to have junk food in the house and she monitored the size of each of our portions. I don't remember her ever being overweight, yet her fear of losing control and gaining weight permeated our house."

In assessing parenting styles and their relationship to appearance obsession, a number of patterns emerge. One of the strongest is the direct link between the importance of looks within the family and the extent to which parents try to influence their children in this arena. When parents care a great deal about their children's looks, they are likely to invest time and energy trying to control or enhance them.

When it comes to eating, however, overinvolvement is likely to backfire. Children naturally rely on hunger and fullness cues to regulate their eating. A study by Dr. Philip Constanzo indicates that when parents step in and exert an influence over their daughter's food intake, she may begin to experience anxiety and guilt about eating, and may begin to distrust her own bodily sensations. In addition, as her eating becomes externally controlled, she may lose her ability to regulate her own eating (see Figure 4.1.).

Figure 4.1.
Consequences Of External Influences On Eating

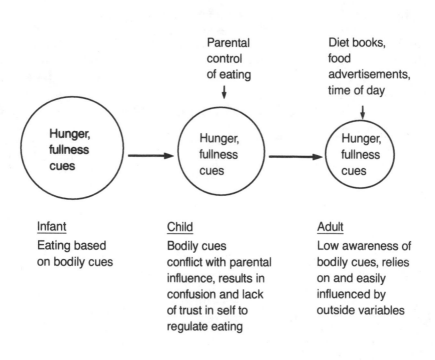

Infant	Child	Adult
Eating based on bodily cues	Bodily cues conflict with parental influence, results in confusion and lack of trust in self to regulate eating	Low awareness of bodily cues, relies on and easily influenced by outside variables

In the short term, eating can become a battlefield within the family — either an all-out war or a secret sabotage. Linda chose the latter; as a child she frequently hid food from her mother and bought forbidden candy bars at recess. As an adult she continued to hide certain foods from her husband. She felt a strong need to eat only very healthy foods in public, and found herself devouring "treats" when she was alone. In the long term, this combination of emotional discomfort about eating, plus a reliance on outside cues for food regulation, placed her at *more* risk for overeating and weight gain.

Whether your mother was overweight, of normal weight or underweight doesn't matter. What does matter, in terms of appearance obsession, is how she felt about her appearance, how she handled these feelings and how much she communicated these concerns to you. As our first role models, moms who continually compare people's looks, who chronically diet and who are running from the beauty shop to the gym are likely to have daughters who compare themselves to others, worry about their weight and rely on exercise to feel good about their appearance.

THE FAMILY BEAUTY CONTEST

Laura is 33 years old, a medical student and recently married. She was raised by her mother and stepfather, and is the oldest of three children. She has a 31-year-old sister and a 27-year-old brother.

Laura describes herself as generally satisfied except for one area — her looks. She has healthy eating habits and exercises regularly; she also feels at ease with her style of dress and has achieved a comfortable balance between a sense of fashion and an awareness of her budget.

Laura's appearance obsession surfaces when she is around attractive women, particularly when her husband is included. She feels threatened and admits that she often avoids social gatherings to circumvent any possibility of arousing painful feelings. Her insecurity around other women has even interfered with her female friendships; Laura talks with shame and embarrassment about an incident where she accused a close friend of "coming on" to her husband at a party. Even now she talks about this event in a self-disparaging manner, yet she feels hopeless to change her feelings in social situations.

Laura's childhood memories center around her sense of inferiority and insecurity in relationship to her sister's appearance. She describes her sister, Dianne, as "the beautiful one" and comments on the numerous comparisons her mother made between her sister and herself. In addition, Laura felt like her father favored Dianne, and as a child Laura directly linked his favoritism to her sister's beauty. Not surprisingly, Dianne also places an extreme emphasis on her looks and has been in treatment for bulimia.

Laura's mother places a strong emphasis on her own appearance too. She has had several plastic surgeries and continues to struggle with the normal changes associated with aging. Laura is close to her mother in many ways, but she also describes a strong sense of competition; for example, Laura recalls a time when her mother would not get her picture made with her daughters unless the photographer assured her that he would retouch the pictures so that all three would appear to be of similar age.

Laura is very attractive, yet she is able to feel good about herself only when she is the most attractive woman in the room. While to some of us the degree of appearance obsession in Laura's family might seem extreme, competition concerning weight and appearance among female siblings, particularly those who are close in age, is common. Parents who compare siblings or who seem to favor a "beautiful" child are likely to heighten sibling competition. While one child may "win" the family beauty contest, both siblings ultimately lose.

Many psychologists talk about the "natural" competition that emerges between mother and daughter as both get older. I don't believe that competition is an inevitable consequence of mother-daughter interactions. Rather, I have observed that mother-daughter competition tends to center around areas in which the mother is dissatisfied with herself.

In the looks arena, this competition can surface in many ways. Many of us observing our mothers struggle with their weight, recall our early resolutions to be different. Our mother may have strongly encouraged us to diet in an attempt to help us, or she may have given us mixed messages about food. When the mother's appearance becomes a source of conflict between parents, the pressure about looks is magnified. And just as our mother's appearance obsession created insecurity, confusion and competition in us, we run the risk of passing it along to our daughters.

WHAT ABOUT DADS?

It's not clear to what extent our fathers (or stepfathers) influence our satisfaction and comfort with our appearance. Research attempts to look at the role of fathers and their impact on women with eating disorders, for example, have yielded mixed results. Dads, more than moms, often play a vital role in communicating gender roles to their children, teaching their daughters what is acceptable behavior for girls and teaching their sons how boys should behave. Some studies suggest that fathers who strongly emphasize traditional sex roles, which inevitably includes messages about "looking pretty" and "acting like a girl," are likely to communicate a high degree of importance about appearance.

Fathers who place a high emphasis on achievement but are emotionally or physically absent may raise a daughter who feels insecure and uncertain of her own self-worth. She may perceive love as conditional upon what she does rather than who she is, and she may find herself continually trying to prove her worthiness to herself and to others. This parenting style, in combination with a father who is critical of or highly invested in his wife's looks, can set the ground for appearance obsession. Laura for instance, recalls her father making frequent comments about her mother's appearance and encouraging her to get plastic surgery as she got older.

TEEN TROUBLE

Messages we receive from peers, teachers, parents and other significant people in our lives become especially important in our teens. As our looks change, so do our perceptions. For many of us, the normal self-focus of teenagers turns into a negative preoccupation with our appearance.

In my survey of 768 men and women, 17 percent of the women and 12 percent of the men felt that they were unattractive teenagers. Adults who believed they were unattractive as teens continue to compare their looks to others as adults. Numerous studies indicate that, because of the intensity of our struggle to achieve a new body image in adolescence, the outcome of this struggle, either positive or negative, travels with us well into adulthood.

Certain factors in adolescence are likely to have influenced the degree to which meeting our society's beauty ideals were important to you. Take the following questionnaire to see how your adolescence may have laid the foundation for appearance obsession.

Adolescent Base For Appearance Obsession

Answer True or False to each of the following questions.

1. _____ I participated in beauty pageants as a teenager or young adult.

2. _____ My parents were comfortable talking about sexual development and the normal changes of puberty.

3. _____ Most of my teenage friends dieted.

4. _____ My teenage years seemed harder for me than for most of my friends.

5. _____ I participated in activities that were weight-conscious (ballet, gymnastics, cheerleading or drill team).

6. _____ I reached puberty earlier than most of my friends.

7. _____ I was considered attractive as a teenager.

8. _____ I started my first diet in my teens.

9. _____ Buying a new outfit was an essential part of important social occasions.

10. _____ I had plastic surgery as a teenager.

11. _____ My complexion as a teenager was about as good as most of my friends.

12. _____ My eating habits were pretty consistent during my teen years.

Scoring: For questions 1, 3, 4, 5, 6, 8, 9 and 10, give yourself one point for each True answer. For every False answer, give yourself a zero. For questions 2, 7, 11 and 12, give yourself one point for every False answer. For every True answer, give yourself a zero.

Add up your total score. In general, the higher your score the more risk factors you encountered in your teen years. In particular, if your score is four or higher, the crucial teen years may have set the stage for a painful relationship with your appearance. This puts you at greater risk for appearance obsession as an adult.

When we consider teenage risk factors, a couple of patterns emerge. In reviewing the questionnaire, you will notice that several of the questions ask how you felt or how you saw yourself in comparison to your friends. Remember how important our friends were when we were teenagers? Without question, as we tackle the dual challenges of figuring out who we are *and* making sure that whoever we are is different from our parents, our friends become our major source of influence and comparison.

Hanging around friends who diet and who equate a new outfit with every social occasion encourages us to do the same. Similarly, while involvement in drill team, cheerleading or weight-conscious sports such as gymnastics or ballet can enhance our popularity and our self-esteem, they can also exacerbate weight concerns. Even today we find a higher incidence of eating disorders among girls who are involved in activities that emphasize slimness.

In reviewing your answers, the key to consider is how your teenage experiences affected *you*. For the few of us who became thinner with puberty, starting puberty early may have been a welcome relief. Sadly, with the "thin-is-in" ideal, most girls who start developing earlier than their friends may develop a high level of body consciousness.

This is because the normal increase in fat that comes with female puberty moves many of us away from today's beauty standards. When our friends still look like little girls but we suddenly develop hips and breasts, we are more likely to see our developing figure as fat or abnormal. This is even more likely to occur when our parents, out of their own discomfort, are not involved in helping us develop an understanding and appreciation of normal sexual development.

Individual Risk: The Depression Connection

Mood swings, confusion and peer pressure are common associations with teen years. Even happy adolescents experience periods of "the blues" for no apparent reason. Looking back on our teen years, most of us can recall minor events that seemed traumatic at the time, and a combined fear and anticipation of growing up. For just a moment, think of a relationship breakup or a disappointment that happened to you as a teenager; even if the event seems silly to you now, I bet that you can still recall the devastation you felt at the time.

Mood swings are relatively normal in teens; depression is not. Teenagers who have an especially hard time may be suffering from an underlying depression that may be masked in the swirl of social activities and school pressures. Many teens are so busy with their outside demands that they lose touch with their inside.

Many teen girls who are perfectionistic and have extremely high expectations of themselves find that activities can begin to distract them from painful feelings. They get caught up in an increasing spiral of activity, lack of self-awareness and a never-ending pressure to perform. With the emphasis on appearance that girls receive, performance pressure invariably includes appearance activities such as dieting, exercise and appearance maintenance. After a while their feelings get focused on their looks. Instead of stress or depression, they feel "fat" or "ugly."

Alternatively, another scenario may develop. A teen girl is unhappy. She feels anxious in social situations, is lonely and doesn't have many friends or dates. With the onset of puberty, her unhappiness becomes focused on her appearance. Maybe she believes that she is overweight (or actually is), is struggling with a problem complexion or focuses on one hated facial feature. Rather than face her underlying unhappiness, she begins to fantasize about how different her life would be if she was "more attractive." This results in a catch-22; she may focus her energy on diet after diet, yet she may also be afraid of changing her appearance out of a concern that her life may not be any better if she succeeds.

On what does she blame her unhappiness then?

Pressure For Boys

Robert's father, an ex-athlete, strongly encouraged his son's athletic participation. From an early age, Robert recalls, his dad practiced football with him and constantly encouraged him to eat. While his father's frequent admonitions to "eat, you know how big those college athletes are" was at times a joke between him and his brother, he also remembers being teased by childhood classmates because he was moderately overweight. Like Linda, whose mother attempted to control her diet, Robert has struggled with food as an adult and notes that he tends to overeat whenever he is stressed or bored.

John, on the other hand, was small as a child and remarked that for a while "I thought skinny was my middle name." When the other boys were reaching puberty, John was still a couple of years away. He strongly felt the discrepancy between his thin frame and the budding masculinity of his peers as he watched the girls in his class go after the taller, bigger boys.

His relationship with his father didn't help. John describes his dad as "very critical," and says that his dad called him a "wimp" whenever he was angry with him. Like Robert, John felt a lot of pressure with athletics, and the disparity between his relatively small size and the performance demands of his early athletic coaches left him feeling inferior and ashamed. Also significant was his father's preoccupation with aging. John remembers his dad's insecurity over his hair loss, his frequent experimentation with hair-replacement products and his face-lift in his middle forties.

As John entered puberty he felt much better about his body and his looks. While puberty usually takes girls farther from the ideal body, it often brings boys closer to the "muscle man" ideal. Because of this we see the opposite risk pattern in boys; boys who start puberty earlier than their peers are likely to have a solid foundation for appearance security. Boys who lag behind may have more trouble developing a firm sense of their masculinity.

How does this affect adult men? John began bodybuilding in his teens and continues to rely heavily on exercise for a positive body image. He feels anxious if he misses one workout and often exercises when injured. In addition, while he is of average size today, he carries around those painful teen memories along with his gym bag. No matter how much he exercises, John continues to compare his looks, particularly his body size and fitness level, to others.

While girls receive attention and pressure about their looks, boys are traditionally evaluated on what they can do. When we consider the spiraling rewards of professional sports, which increasingly demands taller, bigger, more muscle-bound physiques, the boundary between appearance and performance is getting blurred. In addition, the dramatic increase in plastic surgery among men suggests that more and more boys will be exposed to looks-conscious dads.

Figure 4.2. Dual Weight Pressures For Boys

overweight strives to be thinner

underweight strives to be heavier

"Muscle man" Ideal

Here are some childhood risk factors that I have identified for men who are struggling with appearance obsession today:

- being overweight or underweight as a child/teen
- teasing by childhood peers
- family pressure about athletic performance and sports participation

- participation in wrestling, boxing or other "weight-conscious" activities
- family emphasis on looks
- critical, perfectionistic father
- dad who had trouble accepting the physical changes associated with age
- male sibling, close in age, who was better at athletic activities (especially when frequent comparisons were drawn)
- entered puberty later than most peers
- generally considered unattractive as a teen

Exercise: Risk Factors For Men

Go through each of the risk factors and assess to what extent your experiences affected the way you feel about your looks today. Like the exercise for women earlier in the chapter, the purpose of this exercise is to allow you to begin to separate your early body and looks messages from a realistic appraisal of yourself today.

It might be especially helpful to review your relationship with your father and your early messages about athletic performance. Strong messages about sports performance are often so ingrained that the underlying impact on your sense of masculinity can go undetected. Yet, as we observed with John and Robert, the lingering impact on behavior can be strong.

Updating Your Appearance Image

When you look at your personal history of beauty messages, you can begin to let go of your painful childhood memories and begin to form your own appearance image. Reviewing your early beauty messages gives you the opportunity to get a perspective on your appearance. Many of my clients have reviewed childhood and teenage photos to help them get an accurate and objective estimate of how their body looked at different ages.

This review can also help you understand the appearance pressures your parents faced. In reviewing your parents' struggles with weight and age, you may discover that pressures you found hurtful arose from their desire to help you meet society's beauty ideals, a goal that is strongly reinforced in our society.

I would encourage you not only to assess your personal beauty history, but to evaluate your current family interactions involving appearance. Many of us find that even as adults we are particularly sensitive to comments or feedback around looks from our family members. Learning to anticipate, diffuse and respond differently to current beauty messages sends a strong signal to ourselves and to our family that we are taking charge and setting our own appearance standards.

COMMUNICATING WITH YOUR FAMILY
ABOUT APPEARANCE MESSAGES

In the middle of my struggle to get off the diet path, I got together with my family for Thanksgiving. At the airport I was met by my mother, sister, grandmother — and a barrage of comments about my appearance. The ride from the airport included a critique of my sister's (lack of) makeup as well as a brief discussion about whose hair looked better in what style.

During our four-day weekend together, meals were a time of tension and negotiation. Almost every meal included a discussion of the calories of various menu items, problem-solving about ways that we could order what we really wanted to but "make up" for it later on (for example, by skipping dinner), and resolves to "be good" after the holidays. I felt my old dieting mentality kicking into full gear.

Does this sound painfully familiar? Try using the following coping strategies when faced with current family appearance messages.

Anticipate Them

Isn't it odd that even though family communication patterns are highly predictable, they can still take us by surprise? Or that they can still have so much power to (at least temporarily) determine how we feel?

When appearance is an important family value, greetings often include comments about how we look. "Have you gained weight? I liked your hair so much better when it was short. Is that a new outfit?" Even compliments can remind us of the importance of looks in our family, and can cause old appearance insecurities to surface.

One of my clients who only saw her family two or three times a year talked with frustration about the "looks review" a trip home inevitably provoked. When she began to anticipate these comments, she prepared by drawing an imaginary circle around herself. This creative visualization technique helped her to set imaginary boundaries between herself and the looks comments she received, and helped her feel more separate from the family process.

Diffuse Them

As we have seen throughout this chapter, appearance messages are often more about the sender of the message than the receiver. Armed with this knowledge, we can reinterpret comments, criticism or advice as information about our parents or siblings rather than about ourselves. Seeing these old messages in a new light takes away the emotional power we often attach to family feedback about looks and paves the way for reacting differently.

React Differently

How do you react to comments about your looks from your family? Do you get defensive? Do you return the comment with one of your own? When we are caught by family appearance messages, a natural reaction is either to angrily defend ourselves or to respond in kind. Unfortunately, neither of these approaches soothes our emotional reaction (our underlying belief that these comments may be true), and our reaction can actually contribute to the problem.

To determine your best response to ongoing family beauty messages, ask yourself: (1) How often do these messages occur? (2) How much do they hurt my feelings and influence my behavior? (3) What are my options in handling this situation?

When I was trying to get off the dieting treadmill, family messages about food and weight were much harder for me than they are now. During that time, after hearing repeated remarks about my looks at family gatherings, I finally asked my mother not to make comments about my body size or my eating habits. I explained to her that I was having a "hard time" with my eating and that it would help me if she would comply with this request. I had never expressed the impact of her comments before, and while she slipped occasionally, she tried very hard to follow my request. Today she rarely makes such comments, and because I am more secure with my own appearance they have much less impact when she does.

A Final Thought About Our Families

Anticipating appearance comments, and seeing them for what they really are (information about your family's appearance issues rather than a reflection on you), can help you as you begin to work on gaining a personal sense of security and satisfaction about your appearance. If you find that family beauty messages trigger dieting or overexercise, or significantly affect your personal sense of attractiveness for more than a brief time, you may find it helpful to set limits with family members about looks feedback. Rest assured that as you become more satisfied with your appearance and develop a balance between self-acceptance and self-improvement, you will become much less sensitive to lingering family beauty messages.

Now let's see what's happening in the here and now: In Chapter 5, we'll look at the ups and downs of dieting.

DIETING: RIDING THE TRAIN TO THE THIN FARM

I tried the Scarsdale diet, the egg-banana-and-hot-dog diet, the fruit diet. I combined foods, counted calories and chugged water before meals. I dieted before swimsuit season, after holidays and following birthday celebrations. Food was a source of comfort, a relief from boredom and a temporary stress buster. Food also threatened potential weight gain.

From age 21 to age 28, I weighed myself every day. My mood coincided with the numbers on the scale; I felt relief with weight maintenance, alarm with weight gain and satisfaction with a lost pound. I felt "fat" instead of depressed and alternately wore loose or fitted clothes, depending on the reflection that I saw in the mirror. Through my own form of weight control, my eating habits were arbitrarily set by the days on a calender rather than feelings of hunger or fullness. I wasted enormous amounts of energy and effort conforming to this rigid schedule.

As of today I have not dieted in four years. I haven't weighed myself in six months (the last time I went to the doctor), yet I wear the same clothes size today that I wore during my eight years of chronic dieting. The mental battles and emotional turmoil about food are over. I have gradually replaced chronic dieting with natural eating.

In this chapter we will explore the myths and realities of dieting. Most of us think of dieting as a normal activity and, based on the numbers of people who do it, it is. We may dread the process, but we eagerly look forward to the promised reward — weight loss. The relationship between dieting and weight loss, however, is much more complicated and much less direct than we might think. In fact, before we cut back on our calories once more let's look at what dieting will really do for us.

Exercise: Your Diet History

Before you read the rest of this chapter, think about your last diet. Take a sheet of paper and answer the following questions:

1. What prompted your decision to diet? For example, was it inspired by:

- an upcoming social event
- a teasing comment
- swimsuit season
- insurance against upcoming holidays
- a relationship breakup

2. How did you motivate yourself during your diet? Did you promise yourself new clothes, imagine the positive reaction of others, make plans that were dependent upon weight loss?

3. How did you feel when you were on it? Did it affect your mood, your energy level, your relationships with others? If so, how?

4. How long did your diet last? Did you lose weight? If so, have you kept the weight off. If not, what happened?

5. How many diets have you been on?

Add to your answers any emotional and physical consequences you have experienced as a result of dieting. Keep these answers beside you as you read. Relate your answers to this exercise to the information presented.

What's Normal?

Where do you fall on the dieting continuum? Answer True or False to the following questions to find out.

1. ___ I am presently dieting.

2. ___ I diet at least once a month.

3. ___ I weigh myself at least once a day.

4. ___ I feel better about myself when I am on a diet.

5. ___ I know how many calories I have eaten today.

6. ___ I feel guilty when I have eaten certain foods.

7. ___ I feel hungry most of the time when I am dieting.

8. ___ I believe most women diet.

9. ___ I believe my life would be better if I were thinner.

10. ___ I eat less in front of other people than I do alone.

11. ___ I believe there are "good" foods and "bad" foods.

12. ___ I "feel fat" when I am depressed.

13. ___ I believe I have control over how much I weigh.

14. ___ If I had three wishes, losing weight would be one.

15. ___ I frequently eat when I am not hungry.

If you answered True for ten or more of these items, you are in the normal range. In fact, if you are a woman between the ages of 19 and 39, you almost certainly want to lose weight. You may even want to lose weight more than you want a date or a job promotion — most women do! Regardless of your actual weight, you are likely to participate in some form of a diet at least one week out of four. You have a one in six chance of falling into the "constantly dieting" group.

Normal Isn't The Same As Healthy

As a society we think of dieting as normal. We label weight concerns as socially desirable and applaud dieters for their will-power and self-control. We temporarily replace the dissatisfaction we feel toward our bodies with the comfort that "at least I'm doing something about it." We accept many of the painful consequences of the thin-is-in ideal, even those that are so extreme that psychologists initally believed they only occurred in eating disordered patients. Many of these, we are now finding, are common among women in general, and dieting women in particular.

The fear of being fat, for instance, is so common among women that it is no longer viewed as a red flag for an eating disorder. Anorexic women and healthy women *do not differ* in the degree to which they say they are "always on a diet." In my research 37 percent of the women and 24 percent of the men had been on a diet over the past month. Twenty-seven percent of the female respondents and 17 percent of the males dieted at least one week out of every month. How many women do you know who are either on a diet, ending a diet, breaking a diet or gearing up for one?

Most women describe a constant battle of willpower in their relationship with food and believe that hunger is a disgusting attribute. Most women and men overestimate their body size. We are now identifying the pain and frustration that chronic dieters face.

The Truth About Dieting

On the surface, dieting appears to be a successful way to cope with our society's appearance obsession. It makes sense that dieting is a popular way to conform to the thin ideal. As women, we see dieting as a productive behavior — restricting our food intake for the purpose of weight loss. We often overlook the unhealthy physical and emotional consequences of dieting. We attribute success (weight loss) to our diets and failure to ourselves (our "lack of willpower," "poor motivation" or "lack of self-control"). The reality is dramatically different. Chronic dieting is emotionally draining, mentally sabotaging and physically ineffective. Chronic dieting does not work.

THE EMOTIONAL CONSEQUENCES

Laura is a 31-year-old real estate broker. She came to see me because she wanted to feel better about her looks. Most of her dissatisfaction had to do with her body size.

While she had never been overweight, Laura had dieted off and on since high school. For many years she had been determined to wear a size four and she had done so — several different times, for only a few weeks. Once she discontinued her diet, her body naturally settled into a size eight.

Laura had lost more pounds than she could remember. She was tired of her constant fight with food, yet she realized that weight loss had come to symbolize many important goals and dreams to her. Her emotions tended to mirror the "success" or "failure" of her diets. "When I'm losing weight, I feel like I'm doing something for myself. In a way it's like taking care of myself or like an investment in the future — you know, 'When I lose a few pounds I'll feel better and look better.' I imagine the way I'm going to look and the way my life will improve. I picture myself taking charge of situations. I've never thought about it before, but I think I come across as more confident when I start a diet, even before I've lost any weight. Of course, when I blow it, or regain the weight that I've lost, I'm back to square one."

Even if the onset of a diet gives us a temporary boost, the deprivation we impose on ourselves takes its toll. We may feel good about our progress during our diet, yet our hunger and low energy level also leave us feeling overly emotional and moody. Food deprivation keeps our bodies in a constant state of stress. And over time, self-starvation leaves us feeling emotionally deprived. We snap at friends and are easily frustrated. We have trouble concentrating at work; many studies show that dieters tend to be more easily distracted by noises in their environment than nondieters. So the diet itself puts us under emotional stress.

If we discontinue our diet before we reach our "goal weight," we feel frustrated and guilty. We have "failed." We beat ourselves up for our perceived shortcomings. We tell ourselves that we will never lose weight. We berate ourselves for our "weakness." If we diet and regain the weight enough times, we begin to experience a profound sense of failure and helplessness, two emotions that are road signs on the path to depression (see Figure 5.1.).

Take a minute and look back over your answers to the exercise at the beginning of the chapter. How did you feel before, during and after your last diet? How did the physical effects of dieting affect your mood? The sense of control, the emotional highs and the elation of success that we typically attribute to diets are temporary illusions. They are *part* of the dieting picture — along with ongoing hunger, fatigue and irritability. The resulting frustration when the initial weight loss stalls, and the sense of failure when weight is inevitably regained, are as much a part of the dieting process as the short-term highs. When we overlook this, we give our diets too much credit for our successes and ourselves too much blame for our relapses.

Figure 5.1.
Emotional Consequences Of Dieting

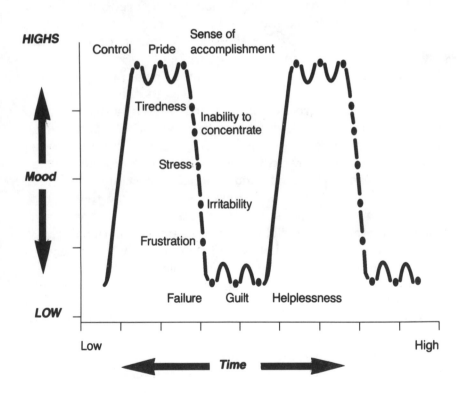

Physical Realities About Body Size

Laura, like most of us, believes that weight is completely a matter of self-control. No matter what her body tells her by continually resuming its natural shape, she doesn't listen. When we accept total responsibility for our body size, we set ourselves up for disappointment and failure. "I am totally in charge of my weight." "It's a matter of willpower." "Diets work if I stick with them long enough." "I can be any size and shape I want if I work hard enough." We're telling ourselves things that aren't true.

Over 20 years ago, a man named Richard Nisbett began pointing out the strong links between heredity and weight. He proposed the "set-point" theory of weight regulation, a theory that continues to gain increasing support. This theory clearly states that a person's natural weight is, for the most part, biologically determined, and any attempt to maintain a weight below this "set-point" will set off an army of bodily defenses determined to counter this attack. One of these defenses is a lowered metabolism, which ultimately sabotages any long-term weight loss and may actually precipitate weight gain.

In Laura's case, her natural body size was a size eight. Her normal weight was approximately 20 pounds heavier than her ideal figure. The more she attempted to push and mold her body into an unnatural shape, the more it fought back. The more she dieted, the more her body slowed down to compensate for her reduced food intake. When she came to see me, she was slightly heavier than she had been *prior to* starting her first diet.

Consider the outcome of a diet. Dieting, by its very nature, starts off with relatively easy weight loss. During the initial period, the dieter feels a sense of accomplishment, control and pride as she learns to ignore bodily cues of hunger. She begins to see pounds come off the scale.

Sooner or later, though, her metabolism begins to slow down, and she experiences frustration as the same efforts do not bring the same rewards. At first she was losing two to three pounds a week. Now she finds herself at the same weight for three weeks in a row. Or she cuts back dramatically for a week before a special occasion, only to find that she quickly regains it after the event, a pattern that has occurred over and over. It gets harder to stick to her diet, and the physiological changes that have occurred make it that much more difficult, particularly if she "slips" and eats something she really enjoys.

If she is "successful" in her initial goal, the odds are over 90 percent that she will regain this weight within five years. Even if she has not lost much weight, she has lowered her metabolism by restricting her food intake. While her metabolism will readjust within two to six weeks, it may still be lower than it was originally. As a result, it may be harder for her to lose weight successfully in the future (see Figure 5.2.).

Figure 5.2.
Physical Consequences Of Dieting

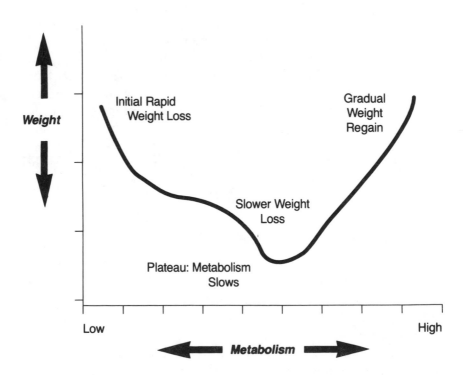

Place a mark on the graph in Figure 5.2 that best represents where you *currently* see yourself. Where would your mark be if you had done this exercise three months ago? Six months ago? Plotting these three time periods on the graph will give you an idea of where you are in the dieting process. It can also help us see the reality of dieting — dieting may temporarily control our eating, but it is much less likely to help us control our weight.

The Dieting Mentality

Dieting isn't just a way of eating or *not* eating. It's also a way of thinking. As dieters we think of calories instead of taste: "I'll have a baked potato and a peach for dinner because I'm allowed 400 calories." We make deals with ourselves: "If I don't eat anything all day, I can eat a lot for dinner tonight." We play food games with ourselves. "I can have two drinks, but that means I'll have to skip dinner." We learn a lot of rules about eating.

One of the first rules of dieting is "You can't trust your body." In order to be "successful" we must ignore those rumblings in our stomachs. Physical signs of hunger and fullness are obstacles rather than eating guidelines. If we are battling our bodies' natural weight in order to conform to a beauty standard, our bodies become our enemies. We must be alert or our bodies will cause us to gain weight. We have to develop a way to "control" these physical guidelines. Cognitive or mental controls take the place of these natural physical controls. "I can only eat 1,200 calories a day." "I don't want to be fat. Summer's coming and I have to fit into that swimsuit." "If I eat that, I'll blow it."

The more we can ignore those hunger pangs, the easier dieting will be. Strict rules and guidelines are substituted for internal signals, and eating becomes regulated by numbers on a scale or calories in a diet book. Our bodies, of course, don't trust us either. Since we are programmed to a certain natural or biological weight, they begin to save fat as soon as we force our bodies below that level.

Our dieting mentality, which we create in an attempt to make dieting easier, is actually a double-edged sword. It influences our behavior in ways that ultimately sabotage our initial goal — that of taking control of our eating. When we listen to our minds instead of our bodies, our control over food is fragile indeed!

When we were babies, our parents relied on us to let them know when we were hungry and when we were full. We cried for a bottle and quit drinking when we'd had enough. As children, we listened to our tummies for information. As dieting adults, we learn to ignore these physical cues, which leaves us more dependent on situational and mental cues — cues that are less stable and easily manipulated. Once these arbitrary controls are broken, we are likely to overcompensate for our physical deprivation by overeating. The price of undereating, ironically, is likely to be overeating.

The second belief we embrace is that we are either being "good" or "bad." There's no such thing as the middle ground. Think of the terms we use to describe dieting. We are either on or off one. We break it or blow it. We succeed or fail. Right now, think of a list of good foods. Are the good foods healthy? Maybe. Are they low in calories or "diet foods"? Of course. Most of us have no problem identifying good foods. What came to mind for you — celery, salads, fruit, fish, nonsweetened juices, carrots, baked potatoes? I bet your list didn't contain ice cream, cookies, nuts or other high-calorie foods. We all know those are in the bad category. For us dieters these are forbidden.

Remember when you were young and you wanted to go across the street and play with a friend? What happened if your mother said "no"? Didn't you suddenly want to go play more than anything in the world?

As adult dieters, we aren't that much different. Foods that we see as forbidden tend to assume a position of power. If we see chocolate cake as a food that is not necessarily a healthy food but one that tastes good and is occasionally enjoyable, we are likely to eat it accordingly. That is, we may eat it on special occasions and do without it most of the time. Or we may order it regularly and have two or three bites.

However, when we see chocolate cake as strictly off-limits, this food takes on magical properties. We may use it to rebel or eat it when we are angry and fed up with "being good." We may use it to soothe hurt feelings. We may eat it to celebrate a special occasion. If eating this food means breaking the rules, then this activity has less to do with physical hunger than it does with other reasons. The problem is that the more we associate our eating patterns to things other than physical hunger, and the more we use food to satisfy other needs temporarily, the less we are able to respond to trustworthy bodily cues. We have arbitrarily assigned important qualities to eating this food, and because of their emotional significance we may have difficulty stopping once we have started.

The Dieter's Dilemma

A friend of mine is famous for her "starting the diet on Monday" ravings. This speech occurs whenever she is eating something that she feels guilty about, usually on the weekend. The words appear when she is looking for justification in eating a second or third cookie. As she says, "What the hell, I've already blown it today, so I might as well enjoy the weekend."

My friend laughs at the irrationality of this logic, but she follows it nonetheless. "How often do I let myself eat things like chocolate cake? Once I start I remind myself that this is a special treat and I'm going to have to make up for it the next day. While I'm using self-talk to try to control myself, sometimes I think my body listens and responds with urgency. I end up eating enough cake for *both* days instead of one."

Imagine that you and a friend have agreed to take part in an experiment. When you get to the testing room, both of you are told that you will be taking part in an ice cream tasting experiment. In addition, you are asked to drink two milkshakes before the ice cream tasting begins, with the explanation that the experimenter wants to see how the taste of the milkshakes affects your response to the ice cream. Going along with the experiment, you drink both of them. Your friend, on the other hand, was taken immediately into the ice cream tasting room. Both of you are offered unlimited amounts of ice cream. Who eats the most ice cream?

Researchers who actually created the above scenario found that the answer to who consumed the most ice cream depended on the person's dieting history. Dieters ate more food when they had been forced to break their diet and consume two milkshakes prior to an alleged ice cream tasting experiment than when they had consumed *no* milkshakes in the precondition. Nondieters, on the other hand, responded to "full" cues and ate small amounts of ice cream after they had consumed milkshakes. When questioned, dieters stated that they felt like they had "already blown it" in the precondition and indulged in the actual experiment. My friend who eats enough chocolate cake for two days is in good company!

Dieting, not weight, was the differentiating factor in subjects who overate in response to a variety of outside influences. Overweight nondieters ate no more than normal weight dieters. If we chronically diet, we are likely to respond with food to emotional stress, alcohol consumption, appealing visual displays of food and many situations in which we believe we have already blown our diet. These studies confirm what most of us, as dieters, know intuitively: we think *more* about food when we're on a diet and are *more* likely to respond to temptations. Figure 5.3 illustrates the dieter's dilemma.

Dieting Leads To Binging

Pat, a successful 35-year-old woman, describes her diet history. "At age 30 I had to stop exercising for a while due to a knee injury. I gained a couple of pounds, not much, but I started feeling afraid that I was going to keep gaining. You know the old saying about your body slowing down with age! For the first time, I went on a diet, mainly as a preventative measure. I never had a weight problem and always considered myself to be fairly thin. I had certainly never dieted before. It was one of the most frustrating experiences I ever had, and eventually led to a four-year struggle with my weight.

"I had always relied on feelings of hunger and fullness to guide my eating. It was extremely difficult for me to ignore the hunger pangs when I first started my diet. In fact, I started and stopped it several times. I did lose the weight; in fact, I lost it many times because I always gained it back plus another five pounds!

"I would find myself daydreaming about food when I was on a diet. I would gaze longingly and, I have to admit, somewhat resentfully at people who were eating desserts or other forbidden foods. Of course, when I went off my diet, I would sooner or later find myself splurging on all those foods that I had deprived myself of, and beating myself up for my lack of willpower."

Figure 5.3. The Dieter's Dilemma

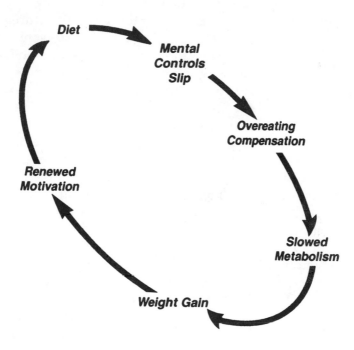

Pat did not begin dieting because her weight put her at medical risk. In fact, her weight was well within normal limits. She began the dieting process out of fear that she would *become* overweight. Laura, the endless seeker of a size four we met earlier, did not have a weight problem. Rather, she was attempting to mold her body to fit the beauty standards. As a result she ended up *gaining* weight.

Because of the unrealistically thin body standards for women, dieting often has to do with appearance, not health, and with fashion, not medicine. It has less to do with actual weight than with a woman's perception of her weight and the degree to which she is dissatisfied with her body. A chronic dieter may be thin, average-sized or overweight. Dieting has become a socially acceptable effort to conform to a certain culturally determined body shape.

The problem with this "solution" is that eventually it creates more problems. During my weekday routine of dieting, I fantasized about the foods I would eat on the weekend. I dreamed about chocolate chip cookies and Chex mix, foods that were strictly taboo during the week. When I overate on the weekend, this confirmed to me the necessity of my strict dieting routine. "See, you have no control over your eating. Think what you'd look like if you ate like this all the time." It never occurred to me that my overeating could be a response to my dieting.

Recent research findings suggest that dieting leads to binging, not the other way around. Most eating-disordered patients do not have a history of obesity prior to their development of an eating disorder. Estimates among non-eating-disordered individuals who engage in some form of binging on a regular basis run as high as 67 percent. Most of them are not overweight. What do they have in common? Bingers are dieters. More important, dieters are bingers — and they begin dieting before they start binging.

When we deprive ourselves over a period of time, we place ourselves at high risk for overeating. Whenever we are eating past the point of physical hunger, we are "binging." The link between dieting and binging is so strong that giving up dieting may actually lead to giving up binging. Dr. Emily Fox Kales, Director of the Eating Disorders Clinic at Harvard's MacClean Hospital, reported an 80 percent reduction in binge eating after taking an antidiet approach with 2,000 patients.

A binge can take many forms. For one of my friends it means eating dessert after every meal on the weekend in preparation for the Monday diet. For a survey respondent it means letting go of her incredibly strict eating schedule and ordering pizza late at night (after dinner) to get through final exams. For an eating-disordered client it means making the rounds of fast-food restaurants and eating herself into a stupor. While the severity of these binges varies, each of these women is compensating for a pattern of chronic deprivation.

The Special Risks Of Cosmetic Dieting

At least 50 percent of all dieters are motivated by cosmetic, not health, reasons. They are dieting in an attempt to look better rather than feel better. And recent research indicates that the less weight we actually need to lose, like those last five to ten pounds, the more dieting works against us.

Here's how:

1. If we are of normal weight, or are mildly to moderately overweight, we are more likely to lose lean muscle tissue while dieting and replace it with fat when we regain the weight. And, remember, there is a better than 90 percent chance that we will regain any lost weight within two to five years.
2. Repeated dieting may also make it more difficult to stick to a maintenance plan after we have lost weight. Some studies indicate that appetite significantly increases following a period of food deprivation, and have noted that fluctuations in weight often lead to cravings for foods high in sugar and fat.
3. A study of 3,130 men and women found that yo-yo dieters had a 70 percent higher risk of heart disease than did people whose weight remained fairly constant, even if they were constantly overweight.
4. A two-year study of dieters and nondieters found consistent eating differences between the two groups — but not consistent weight differences. In other words, dieters tended to keep dieting but did not lose more weight.

The No-Diet Strategy: Natural Eating

Chronic dieting does not work. It results in physical and emotional chaos. The temporary success of weight loss is soon counterbalanced by the frustration of weight gain. The highs of motivation and enthusiasm are replaced by the lows of disappointment and self-criticism. Instead of a model's figure, a lowered metabolism and an ongoing sense of frustration are the typical prizes in the dieting game.

Does that mean weight loss is impossible? As we have seen, there are indisputable genetic constraints that highly influence our body size. As in Laura's case, if our body is a natural size eight, we may temporarily starve ourselves into a size four, but it will be extremely difficult to maintain it. And unless we are at least 30 percent over a "normal" weight for our age, sex and height, or are suffering from weight-related medical problems, the facts suggest that we might be better off accepting our bodies the way they are — and learning to trust them, rather than the cultural beauty ideals, to guide our eating.

SIX STEPS TO NATURAL EATING

Step 1. Understanding Your Relationship With Food

Natural eating means responding to physical needs for food rather than to emotional needs. A first step in this process is to understand your present relationship with food and identify trigger situations that influence your eating. Use the checklist below to mark situations that disturb your eating. Put a check by any situation that routinely affects your eating. If you have trouble answering, keep a written record of your eating habits for two weeks. You will begin to see patterns that may surprise you.

As you are answering the questions, try to identify patterns in your relationship with food. Put a "D" beside the questions that trigger dieting and an "O" by situations that often result in overeating.

Disordered Internal Eating Test (DIET)

1. ____ When I've had too much alcohol to drink.

2. ____ When food is easily available.

3. ____ At meal times (noon, 6:00 P.M.) whether I'm hungry or not.

4. ____ When I've had an argument with someone.

5. ____ When I'm bored.

6. ____ When I've already eaten something high in calories.

7. ____ When I'm on a date.

8. ___ When I'm around attractive women.

9. ___ After stressful job or school situation (test, job presentation, etc.).

10. ___ When I'm watching TV or reading.

11. ___ When I'm feeling "down in the dumps."

12. ___ When I see food commercials or advertisements.

13. ___ When I'm starting a diet the next day.

14. ___ On weekends.

15. ___ When I'm celebrating a special occasion.

16. ___ When I'm visiting my family.

17. ___ Before or after weighing myself.

18. ___ When I'm "feeling fat."

19. ___ Before or after trying on clothes.

20. ___ When I've missed exercising that day.

21. ___ After a relationship breakup.

22. ___ When I feel sexually frustrated.

What patterns emerge? How do you use food, or diets, as a Band-Aid? Do you eat when you are tired, bored, angry? Do you start a diet to gain a sense of control or when your social life is in the dumps? What emotional needs are you ignoring? For example, if you find yourself eating like a bird in front of a date so he won't think you're a "pig," maybe you're looking for approval instead of weight loss. Listen to your emotional hunger and develop alternate behaviors to meet these needs.

Part of understanding our relationship with food means identifying our own way of binging. Just as certain situations are likely to trigger dieting, other situations tempt us to overindulge, particularly if we have been dieting. What is food giving you in that situation — comfort, pleasure, relief from boredom or stress? Once you identify the emotional need that is being temporarily met with food, you can begin to identify other ways to meet these needs. For example, if you use food to distract you from boredom, what can you do to make your life more exciting? If food brings you comfort, what else can you use to comfort yourself?

One of my clients, Christi, in analyzing her DIET inventory, came up with the following analysis:

Trigger Situation	Emotional Need	Response
weekends	excitement/pleasure	overeat
job stress	comfort	overeat
weighing	self-esteem, acceptance	diet/undereat
date	acceptance, approval	undereat
arguments/conflict	security/reassurance	overeat

Christi began to identify ways she used food to meet other needs. Then she listed other ways to meet her emotional needs. She started planning non-eating-related activities on the weekend — activities that were new and exciting to her. She began engaging in self-nurturing activities when she needed comfort and reassurance; instead of cookies, she gave herself a bubble bath or flowers. She realized that a diet symbolized acceptance, approval and self-control. She began working on her self-esteem instead of her weight.

Another client, Suzanne, is a successful 28-year-old attorney who manages her life with a calendar, a car phone and a traveling gym bag. She exercises three times a week, consistently, at the same class, on the same days and at the same times. Her life is organized, hectic and, for the most part, enjoyable. Yet, during a therapy session, she described her eating style as chaotic and inconsistent. She was unable to see patterns of disturbed eating. Instead, she initially attributed her dietary chaos to a demanding schedule and a pressing weight concern.

Going through the DIET exercise, Suzanne began to realize that her disordered eating had definite patterns. She identified several recurring situations that triggered overeating, as well as events that almost always triggered a new diet. "I had never realized how routine my disturbed eating had become. I was constantly vowing to lose weight and constantly making deals with myself. I was such an emotional eater — starving myself while I was getting ready for a trial and then splurging to celebrate its end. I was dieting either to impress a new boyfriend or in the hopes of getting one. I was a seasonal eater; every summer I went on a crash diet and every winter I gave myself permission to indulge over the holidays."

Recognizing these patterns and their underlying emotional needs gave Suzanne and Christi the chance to take control over their eating and to permanently address their emotional hunger. We may still splurge at a holiday party, or celebrate a success by treating ourselves to a fudge sundae; we all need the freedom to indulge occasionally. Separating emotional needs from physical needs simply insures that eating no longer becomes a routine (and temporary) substitute for important emotional needs such as comfort, nurturance or pleasure.

Step 2. Reacquaint Yourself With Physical Cues

For the next two weeks, focus on your physical sensations of hunger and fullness. Listen to the rumblings in your stomach and the hollow feeling that lets you know that you are physically hungry. Eat a small amount of food when you recognize these signals, and then stop. Wait a few minutes before you resume eating. Notice the impact your food has on your hunger sensations.

Many of us find that fullness is a more difficult sensation to relearn than hunger. Satisfaction is a lot more subtle than "stuffed"; when I first began natural eating, the two were hard to distinguish. Making "positive deals" with myself helped me learn satisfaction cues. I would eat a certain amount of food and then wait for ten minutes. During this waiting period I would reassure myself that if I was still hungry, I would continue to eat. Making this deal over a period of time worked — somehow having the emotional "permission" to eat freed me to focus on my physical sensations.

In learning to eat naturally, Suzanne first began to pay attention to signs of hunger. She noticed that her stomach felt hollow and empty if she went without food for five hours or more. She noted her emotional response to food deprivation — she consistently became irritable and snapped at others when she was hungry. She also found herself thinking about food when she had not eaten.

Next, she learned to get in touch with "I'm satisfied" cues from her body. This was somewhat more difficult, as Suzanne was used to feeling "stuffed" after splurging. Satisfaction was a more subtle cue. She experimented with her food; she negotiated with herself and, like me, gave herself permission to eat more if she didn't feel satisfied after eating. Most of the time she didn't eat more.

Natural eating is a simple process that, for us chronic dieters, can initially seem as foreign as a new language. Because we have unlearned many of the basics, it can also be frightening to trust our bodies rather than a diet book or calorie counter. Having a friend go through the process with you can help alleviate some of the initial anxiety. Here are two tips that can help you tune into your body:

(1) *Pay attention to your food.* Engaging in other activities while you are eating is a setup; it distracts you from the amount that you eat and takes away the enjoyment of what you are eating. Make a pact with yourself to sit down while you are eating and to concentrate only on the taste of the food and your body's response to it. Don't read a book, watch TV or engage in any other activity during your meal.

(2) *Don't skip meals.* Your body generally needs food every five hours. Skipping meals causes your body stress and makes it harder to identify bodily signals. This is particularly true in the morning, a time when many of us find it easy to do without food and are less sensitive to hunger cues. Many of my clients who are adamant about their lack of hunger in the morning tended to overeat at night. Yet, when they began breakfast on a regular basis, they began to wake up hungry — and spontaneously found themselves eating less later in the day.

Step 3. Change Your Dieting Mentality

Stopping your dieting behavior can be easier than turning off your dieting mentality. For months, a mental calorie counter accompanied me to every meal. I found myself automatically adding up my calories as I was eating, while a little gremlin interpreted the results for me in terms of potential weight loss or weight gain! After all those years of calorie monitoring, it took a lot of work *not* to think of food in terms of calories and pounds. While these old messages occasionally surface even today, they have much less impact than they used to. How did I change my calorie counter? By literally telling myself "stop" when this process began and by gently redirecting my thoughts to the enjoyment of my meal and the physical cues of my body — over and over again.

Changing your dieting mentality also means getting rid of your judgmental dieting vocabulary — terms like "good" and "bad" foods. While certain foods are more or less healthy, no foods are harmful if eaten in moderation. When we have the freedom to eat whatever we want, we find that the taste, rather than the amount, of a desired food becomes more important. Remember the "What the hell, I've already blown it so I might as well go ahead and splurge" phenomenon? We are much less likely to eat four pieces of cake if we know we can have a bite anytime.

Step 4. Give Less "Weight" To Weight

Because weight carries so much importance in our society, our satisfaction with our weight can directly affect our behavior. In my research, 27 percent of the women and 16 percent of the men said they found themselves putting off plans until they lost weight. Twenty-seven percent of the women had used diet pills and 37 percent had dieted in the past month.

The more we focus on our weight, the less satisfied we are with it. Giving less "weight" to weight means taking away the power we give to numbers. One in every five of my survey respondents, both men and women, stated that they weighed themselves one or more times a day. If our mood depends on the numbers on our scale, even our normal weight fluctuations may trigger an emotional rollercoaster ride.

There are better and more reliable ways to keep track of our body size than the bathroom scales. Begin using a favorite outfit as a measure of your body size. If weighing yourself is something you aren't ready to give up, *don't* weigh yourself more than once every two weeks, and establish an acceptable weight range.

The U.S. Department of Agriculture and the Department of Health and Human Services recently revised its figures regarding healthy weights for men and women, as shown in Table 5.1. Use these as guidelines in establishing an acceptable range for yourself.

Note: these figures allow a 30-pound weight range for each height. If only we could be so flexible with ourselves.

Table 5.1. Revised Government Figures For Healthy Weights For Men And Women (Weight in Pounds)		
Height	19 to 34 years	35 years and older
5'0"	97-128	108-138
5'1"	101-132	111-143
5'2"	104-137	115-148
5'3"	107-141	119-152
5'4"	111-146	122-157
5'5"	114-150	126-162
5'6"	118-155	130-167
5'7"	121-160	134-172
5'8"	125-164	138-178
5'9"	129-169	142-183
5'10"	132-174	146-188
5'11"	136-179	151-194
6'0"	140-184	155-199
6'1"	144-189	159-205
6'2"	148-195	164-210

Step 5. Exercise Moderately

Use moderate exercise to improve your fitness level, muscle tone and flexibility. Moderate exercise can energize a sluggish metabolism and can be particularly helpful if you have a history of yo-yo dieting. Make plans, regardless of your current weight, and keep them! In short, focus on aspects of your body (and your life) that you do have control over rather than agonizing over those you don't.

Step 6. Form An Antidiet Support Group

Antidiet support groups are on the rise. Several dozen health maintenance organizations and corporate health plans have discontinued traditional weight-loss programs in favor of an antidiet approach that encourages healthy eating, moderate exercise and weight maintenance. The result — many programs report a dramatic decrease in binge eating and an increase in weight maintenance and personal satisfaction!

Addicted To Dieting?

Valerie, a 21-year-old model, started dieting when she was told by an agency that she needed to lose a few pounds for a swimsuit shoot. She had exercised regularly for several years and her healthy lifestyle had resulted in a well-toned and attractive body shape. She was naturally tall and slightly built, and had never focused on her weight in spite of her profession.

Dieting was a new experience and a relatively easy one. Valerie quickly learned to ignore hunger pangs and soon began to like the "hollow" feeling in her stomach. She began to associate feelings of hunger with a sense of lightness and well-being. As her weight dropped, she felt euphoric over her success and basked in the knowledge that she had lost more weight than was originally requested. In a profession as competitive as modeling, she viewed this as a "cushion" against possible relapse and weight gain.

Soon, however, Valerie began getting negative feedback about her weight from her modeling agent. This time the message was to gain weight. Valerie was aware that her weight was getting dangerously low. On one level she was concerned and began monitoring her weight in an attempt to regain some weight. At the same time, she continued to be secretly pleased when she maintained her low weight or even lost a few more pounds. She did not see herself as fat or exhibit other signs of an eating disorder. She had simply learned to ignore physical cues and to associate eating with physical discomfort and heaviness. She had become addicted to dieting.

Dieting And Eating Disorders

The exact relationship between dieting and eating disorders is unclear, even to medical professionals. However, there is unquestionably a strong link. Most dieters do not develop an eating disorder. At the same time, eating disorders occur *only* in countries that promote a thin body ideal for women. A thin ideal is a clear precipitant for dieting. In fact, studies among a variety of countries indicate that these two variables — a thin body standard and the incidence of eating disorders — always co-exist.

It is important to be aware of red flags that signal the potential crossover from disordered eating, such as chronic dieting, to an eating disorder. The primary difference between my eating-disordered clients and chronic dieters is the severity of the behavior. That is, eating-disordered clients fall at the extreme end of the eating continuum (see Table 5.2.).

Table 5.2. The Eating Continuum

Healthy Eating	Disordered Eating	Eating Disorders
• eating based on physical cues of hunger/fullness	• eating based on mental or situational cues • dieting	• disordered eating resulting in weight loss or gain of 15 percent of normal body weight

As we have seen, the primary distinction between healthy eating and disordered eating are the cues you use. If you eat when you are physically hungry and stop when you are full *most* of the time, you fall toward the healthy end of the spectrum. If you diet at least once a month, you fall in the disordered-eating range. Most women fall somewhere between normal and disordered eating.

Do You Have An Eating Disorder?

The following questions will assist you in distinguishing between disordered eating and an eating disorder.

1. ____ Have you lost or gained 15 percent of your total body weight in the past year?

2. ____ Have you experienced physical problems as a result of weight loss or weight gain? (These include high blood pressure, chronic fatigue, loss of menstrual periods, water retention, stomach pain, hair loss.)

3. ____ Are you getting concerned feedback from friends about your eating habits?

4. ____ Do you use diet pills, laxatives, or vomiting as a routine form of weight control twice a week or more?

5. ____ Do you weigh yourself once a day or more? .

6. ____ Are your eating habits dramatically different in public than they are in private? (For example, do you eat before or after a date and merely pick at your food while on a date?)

7. ____ Do you feel out of control of your eating (either you can't eat or you can't stop once you start)?

8. ____ Do you "binge" (eat well past the point of physical comfort) twice a week or more?

If you answered yes to three or more of these questions, your answers indicate a considerable amount of pain involved with your eating and your weight. Furthermore, your disordered eating may be shifting into the eating-disordered arena. I recommend that you seek additional information or assistance. Consulting one of the eating-disorder associations listed in the Resources at the end of this book is a way to begin taking control of your eating.

A Final Thought About Dieting

Throughout this chapter we have looked at the realities and consequences of dieting. We have seen how a comparison between ourselves and unrealistic beauty standards can easily lead us to believe that we have a weight problem. In a normal attempt to try to "fix" it, dieting seems like a natural solution. Yet the solution is often much more a problem than our weight. After trying many diets, we find that we have the same body size and a larger sense of failure and frustration.

Failing to meet the super-thin ideal is not a weight problem. In fact, unless we are 20 to 30 percent above the weight ranges for our height and age *and* are at risk for weight-related medical problems, *we don't have a weight problem.* As we have seen, dieting for cosmetic reasons may be especially detrimental.

An alternative to dieting is natural eating. We have looked at some specific strategies that will help us eat naturally — by first understanding our relationship with food, feeding our emotional needs (without food!) and getting back in touch with physical sensations of hunger and fullness. We have seen how breaking free of dieting also requires mental work; we stop thinking of "good" and "bad" foods and stop counting calories. We give less power to the scales and more to our internal body signals. As a result we feel more in control of our lives.

EXERCISING TO LOOK GOOD

Sandra is a 23-year-old college student and aerobics instructor. She exercises seven days a week, often for two hours at a time. She has a personal weight trainer, runs and does aerobics.

As an aerobics instructor, Sandra has a reputation of being tough. In fact, even regular exercisers will avoid Sandra's classes because of the difficulty level. While the owner of the club has often asked her to adapt her class to the ability of her students, Sandra has a great deal of difficulty doing so. She painfully admits that her fear of "not getting a good workout" often overcomes her sensitivity to class attendees.

Sandra has tried to cut back on her exercise. When her personal trainer encouraged her to exercise more moderately, she bought a heart monitor to assess her target heart rate and attempted to become more sensitive to the internal cues she had learned to ignore. Yet after a couple of weeks, the heart monitor was gone and Sandra was back to her seven-day-a-week exercise routine.

Exercise Pressures

Many of us, when reading about Sandra, admire her discipline and dedication to her exercise schedule — especially if our exercise routine is a constant battle, which we sometimes "win" and sometimes "lose." With our busy schedules, it is true that making time for exercise often requires a concerted effort. When we see someone who has conquered the scheduling dilemma, we may feel ashamed that we are having difficulty doing so and envious of someone who has. One of my clients ruefully said, "I wish overexercise was my problem." There was a time in my life when I felt the same way.

With the current mandate of fitness in our society's beauty messages, exercise can easily take on too much importance. When we try to evaluate the importance of our exercise routines honestly, our eyes may be blurred by social approval. We would express concern if we saw someone regularly abusing alcohol, yet seeing that same person at the gym for hours at a time is likely to prompt a completely different reaction. Like dieting, exercise has come to mean discipline, willpower and self-control, and excessive exercising may be fueled by glances of admiration and envy.

"Exercise so you can eat more." "No pain, no gain." "Success means fit." These are all messages that we hear everyday. For many of us, they translate into the dangerous adage, "More is better." This chapter will look at the realities of exercise — what exercise can do for us, what it can't and what happens if we do too much.

The Argument For Exercise

There are good reasons to exercise regularly. Study after study supports the benefits of moderate exercise, both in terms of health benefits and psychological well-being. Most of us feel good right after we exercise. We've also heard about the possible benefits of exercise in producing bodily changes that reduce the risk of heart disease, osteoporosis, strokes and diabetes. Moderate- to high-intensity aerobic exercise, for example, lowers blood pressure for two to five hours after we stop; when done consistently it has been found to reduce the overall risk of high blood pressure.

While clear relationships exist between exercise and certain reduced health risks, we are still unclear about the specific physiological benefits of exercise and how they may eventually affect how long we live. However, there is less controversy in the scientific community over the *improved quality of life* that most exercisers report. Most regular exercisers describe a high energy level and a sense of being younger than their chronological age.

There are also clear-cut emotional payoffs. A study by Dr. Tom Stephens found that, based on the reports of consistent exercisers, physical activity was related to a positive mood and fewer feelings of anxiety and depression. Anxiety that is situational, that is, it arises from a specific source such as an upcoming work presentation or speech, is particularly responsive to exercise. Moderate and consistent exercise is particularly helpful as it appears to provide a buffer to everyday stressors.

Moderate exercise also reduces mild to moderate depression; while we may not feel like exercising when we are down in the dumps, most of us know that once we get to the gym we'll be glad we did. Women, particularly older women, report the most positive benefits.

For women in particular, exercise often brings additional psychological benefits. Because we often perceive our bodies in terms of how they *look*, physical activity can help us appreciate how our bodies *work*. We may begin to feel the physical sensations that occur while we are stretching, or notice our coordination on the dance floor. One of my female colleagues who had started a moderate program of weight training commented that for the first time in her life she felt "strong." Watching herself gradually lift more weights gave her a psychological sense of empowerment and strength.

We don't have to exercise for hours at a time, or every day of the week, to reap the rewards of consistent exercise. Exercising for 20 to 30 minutes at a time, three days a week, is enough to see the psychological effects. And even breaking into a sweat once a week may lead to a reduced health risk: in a study of more than 87,000 women, vigorous exercise one day a week cut the risk of adult onset diabetes by one-third.

Will Exercise Help You Lose Weight?

What about exercising for weight control? Most diets today strongly encourage exercise, and people who are working to keep lost weight off usually cite exercise as a major help. Does it work?

The primary benefit of consistent, moderate exercise is that it can raise our metabolism. (Numerous articles have shown how much exercise it takes to burn off various "forbidden treats" and for many the results are depressing. For example, we might have to exercise for an hour to "afford" a few minutes of delicious cookie devouring, a trade-off that doesn't seem fair!) The reason that exercise can promote weight loss is not this straight exercise-for-calories trade, but the impact on our metabolism for the rest of the day. Not only does moderate exercise raise our metabolism while we are exercising, we have an added metabolic boost for several hours after we have finished. So, yes, moderate eating plus moderate exercise give us an edge if we are trying to lose weight.

What about keeping your weight off? Most studies of the role of exercise in weight maintenance have looked at women. The results may surprise you. Yes, women who were able to maintain their weight loss developed a consistent exercise routine and stuck to it. But the type of exercise they did, the number of times a week they did it, and the length of time during each exercise didn't matter. Exercising three times a week for ten minutes was as effective as a five-day-a-week, 30-minute workout in terms of keeping weight off.

These findings may run counter to our intuition — we know that moderate and consistent exercising raises the number of calories we burn. Yet, in this study, physiological changes obviously do not account for the sustained weight loss since the intensity and the frequency of the workout were of no consequence. The secret may be in the act of *regular* exercising. And the secret to regular exercise, in terms of weight maintenance, may lie more in our minds than in our bodies.

Most of us find that when we are in a regular exercise routine, particularly one that we enjoy, we feel better about ourselves. There is a positive relationship between self-esteem and moderate, consistent exercise. Think of what our commitment to moderate exercise says about our belief in our self-worth, particularly when our exercise is motivated by the stress-relief and health-promoting benefits.

When we do things to boost ourselves emotionally and physically, we are consistently telling ourselves about our personal value. We are affirming a commitment to our health, we are proud of it and we are providing a regular outlet for our stress. We are also likely to make better food choices; somehow, when we exercise, our health-promoting attitude seems to spill over into healthier eating habits. Choosing to exercise regularly is likely to result in better choices in other areas.

THE PHYSICAL CONSEQUENCES OF TOO MUCH EXERCISE

In our discussion of exercise, you may have noticed that two words appear repeatedly: *consistency* and *moderation*. When it comes to exercise, these are the keys to receiving the maximum health and emotional benefits. In fact, research indicates that too much exercise may be worse than none at all.

Unfortunately, much less media attention has been given to the potential harm that overexercise can cause, particularly at high levels of intensity. Women whose body weight falls below a certain point can lose their menstrual periods as their bodies attempt to conserve as much energy as possible. I recently overheard a personal trainer warning a gung-ho weightlifter about "overdoing it," saying that he has seen some of his clients get sick from overexertion. Research supports this; overexercise can overtax our bodies and leave us at risk for infections and other ailments. Stories from, and studies of, extreme long distance runners tend to confirm this belief.

There are other dangers with overexercise as well. In spite of her extremely rigorous exercise routine, Sandra constantly watched her food intake, frequently dieted and described herself as someone who easily gains weight. When talking about her exercise pattern, she often justified it by saying, "I have to. I cringe when I think of how big I would be if I didn't exercise so much."

Not necessarily. In Chapter 5 we reviewed the physical consequences of dieting and realized that it can actually promote weight gain. Just as dieting sends starvation cues to our bodies, which respond by slowing our metabolism, overexercise may send similar cues and have similar results (see Figure 6.1.).

Figure 6.1.
Relationship Between Exercise And Metabolism

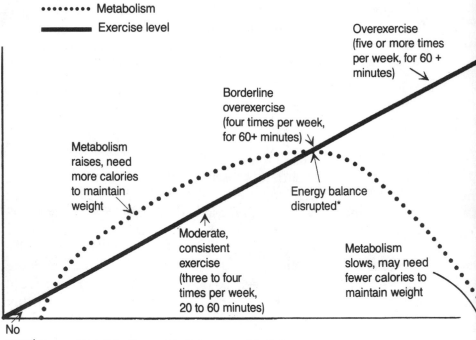

When we disturb our body's balance of energy, it responds by conserving it. This means that we may actually have to eat less to weigh the same if we are exercising too much. Women appear to be especially susceptible to an energy conservation response brought on by overexercise.

Cyclic exercising — starting an exercise routine and stopping it over and over — can produce the same effects as yo-yo dieting. Studies indicate that it may build up body fat or lead to frequent shifts in weight.

LOOKING FIT: A RISKY MOTIVATOR

Do you exercise primarily to improve the way you look? I recently read an article describing "obligatory runners," athletes who felt compelled to keep up their frantic exercise schedule. In our looks-conscious society, who among us doesn't feel obliged to exercise?

In my study, 30 percent of the respondents, both male and female, believe that looking better is the primary motivation for working out. It's certainly true that enjoying the appearance benefits that can come from exercise is a natural result of the fitness addition to our present cultural beauty ideals. When looking good is overemphasized as a motivator for exercise, however, three things can occur.

First, while we are likely to see stress-management benefits right after a workout, it takes a while to see changes in our muscle tone and appearance. When looks are the primary motivator, the chances that we will stick to a regular exercise routine become less.

Second, feeling pressure to exercise for appearance can turn a potentially positive sign of self-care into a chore. Exercise becomes another thing we have to do to keep up with our appearance image. We become focused on the outcome of the exercise, rather than enjoying the process of physical activity. For most of us, chores are a lot harder to complete than something that is fun and helpful!

Third, on an emotional level, exercising for weight and muscle tone sends a strong message to our inner selves about our priorities. Once again, we are saying that the way we look is more important than the way we feel. Studies suggest that our insides are listening; women whose exercise motivation was attractiveness also had lower self-esteem and a higher dissatisfaction with their bodies. They were also more likely to diet and suffer from eating disturbances. Exercising for health and stress relief, on the other hand, was associated with higher self-esteem. When we do things out of a desire to take care of ourselves, we feel better about ourselves.

WHEN EXERCISE TAKES CONTROL

Who's in control, you or your exercise routine? The following questions will help you assess the degree to which your exercise may be getting out of control.

Are You At Risk For Overexercise?

Answer True or False to the following questions.

1. _____ The way my body looks to me depends on whether I have exercised that day or not.

2. _____ I often exercise when I have an injury or don't feel well.

3. _____ For one year or longer, I have exercised five or more times a week for one hour or more.

4. _____ I feel depressed and/or irritable if I miss exercising for three days or more.

5. _____ I find myself continually adding newer and stricter goals to my exercise routine.

6. _____ I will dramatically alter my schedule in order to work out.

7. _____ I feel anxious if I miss even one workout.

8. _____ At times I have used exercise to avoid dealing with work or relationship problems.

9. _____ I often feel like I hate my exercise routine, but feel unable to stop it.

10. _____ I exercise primarily for weight control and muscle tone.

11. _____ I keep detailed records or logs of my workout sessions.

12. _____ It would be very difficult for me to change my exercise. (For example, if you are a runner, you would be unwilling to switch or alternate with aerobic dance or bicycling.)

13. _____ I frequently find myself thinking about exercising in between workouts.

14. ___ While I am exercising, I often find myself daydreaming about
the possibility of a "new, improved" physique.

Scoring: Give yourself one point for every True response. Add up your
total points and see where you fall on the exercise continuum as follows.

0–3: You are normally in control of your exercise schedule. Like many
of us, you may at times have mixed feelings about your exercise schedule
— sometimes enjoying it, sometimes not. It may be helpful to assess
your exercise motivation to see how "looking good" fits in. However,
your answers suggest that you are not presently at risk for overexercise.

4–6: You are in the borderline range of overexercise. It will be important to assess your exercise behavior to see how it may be affecting other
areas of your life. Even if it is not, your pattern of responses suggests
that you are not getting a lot of enjoyment out of your current exercise
pattern. Follow the steps to see how you can change this.

7 or more: You are likely to depend on exercise for a sense of self-
worth. This dependency may cause problems in other areas of your life,
or you may be feeling like your exercise is controlling you rather than
the other way around. Later in this chapter you will find some specific
steps that will help you assess why you are overexercising and what you
can do about it.

When Exercise Is An Escape Strategy

One of my clients, Steve, began exercising more and more as
his marriage deteriorated. Rather than face an uncertain situation
at home, he headed for the gym after work and came home three
hours later. His exercise routine temporarily helped him in two
ways. First, it enabled him to avoid the pain and frustration he
felt at home in a socially acceptable way; after all, who could
criticize his desire to exercise? Second, while he was in the gym,
his workout gave him a short-lived boost in self-esteem. While
he lifted weights he felt powerful.

The problem with these solutions is that they are temporary.
Steve was hurting, and his exercise helped him avoid these feelings rather than understand and deal with them directly. Also, as
Steve spent an increasing amount of time at the gym and away
from home, his exercise routine began to contribute to the tense
situation.

When exercise becomes a *need* rather than a choice, we may be
relying on it to fill empty places in our lives. We may use it to

avoid problems that need to be addressed, or relationships that are frightening or in conflict. There may be worse ways to postpone problem-solving, yet the outcome is the same; the problems or relationship issues are still there when we get back from the gym. Of course, if we make exercise a priority to the extent that work or relationships suffer, eventually we may lose them. Either way, what will remain is a sense of loneliness and frustration coupled with an increasing sense of being out of control as we continue to feel trapped by our rigorous exercise schedule.

When Exercise Signals Appearance Obsession

We can also become dependent on exercise to boost our body image. While moderate exercise is likely to help us feel good about ourselves and our bodies, having to exercise to maintain an acceptable view of our bodies does not. In fact, excessive exercise tends to relate to body dissatisfaction. This is especially true if we feel anxiety or guilt over one missed workout, or if the way we feel about our looks depends on our daily exercise.

An excessive exercise schedule is often a sign of an underlying appearance obsession — and a painful relationship with our bodies. Thirty-four percent of my survey respondents stated that they felt anxious if they missed even one workout, and significantly more men (40 percent) felt this way than women (29 percent). Given the emphasis on muscle mass and fitness with current beauty standards for men, men may be at more risk for excessive exercise than women.

Men and women who felt anxiety about missed exercise were also more likely to avoid social situations if they didn't have the "right outfit." Anxious men reported a higher frequency of binge eating. As the level of exercise increased, so did clothes shopping; men and women who exercised at the highest levels also spent the most money on clothes. Men who exercised the most also reported being more looks-consciousness in public, while high-intensity female exercisers described problematic eating patterns, particularly weekly binges. These findings provide support for an overall problem with looks and a self-improvement coping style. Unfortunately, this coping style does not lead to appearance security.

Taking Control Of Your Exercise

Taking control of your exercise means allowing yourself to experience and enjoy the emotional and physical benefits of exercise. The following strategies are geared toward helping you develop an exercise routine that is moderate and consistent. That may mean re-evaluating the sources of your motivation and making regular exercise more of a priority. Or it may mean taking a close look at an excessive exercise routine and evaluating how it may be hiding problems and even creating some. Let's look at some strategies you can use to optimize your exercise benefits.

LISTEN TO THE EXPERTS (SOME OF THE TIME)

The American College of Sports Medicine recommends exercising at least three times a week for up to 60 minutes at a time. If you are doing aerobic exercise, experts recommend exercising at between 60 to 75 percent of your maximum heart range. Determine your maximum heart range by subtracting your age from 220 and then multiplying that figure by 60 or 75 percent.

Monitoring your heart rate can be a good way to begin getting in touch with your body and its response to exercise. However, once you have done so, I personally prefer the "talk test": Can you carry on a conversation with someone else while you are exercising? Exercise should be comfortable; the old "No pain, no gain" mentality unfortunately still haunts most of us, *despite* increasing evidence that pain should be considered a warning signal, not a sign of accomplishment!

As we have seen, we can get many of the emotional and physical benefits by exercising 20 to 30 minutes, three times a week. But it is less clear at what point exercise becomes counterproductive. Physically, we increase the risk of muscle and joint injuries when we exercise more than three days a week or for longer than 60 minutes at a time. Here's a guideline: if you are exercising for longer than one hour at a time, and particularly if you are exercising longer than one hour five days a week or more, you may be exercising to excess.

EVALUATE YOUR EXERCISE MOTIVATION

"The next time you move, notice how many bones you have that you cannot see. Feel your muscles stretch as you bend . . . Our bodies are miraculous things, and every time we move, it is a celebration — or a prayer."

The above quote came from a Nike commercial. Naturally the product was exercise shoes, and there was a physically fit female model exercising during the commercial. Yet the commercial caught my attention because it focused on how our bodies work, and the many things they do, rather than the all-too-often promises of a better look. Focusing on how our body works gives us a different appreciation of the many things it does every day.

As we have seen, focusing on the appearance aspect of exercise may prevent us from enjoying the exercise itself. One way to begin focusing on the health and psychological benefits of exercise is to pay attention to your body while you are exercising. Rather than rating yourself in the aerobics mirror, or looking to see if that cellulite is going away, focus on your body's movement and coordination. Watch how gracefully you dance, how easily you pick up an aerobic step, how strong you feel. Increasing your body sensitivity not only helps you "see" your body in a new way, it can also reduce the risks of injuries and overexertion. If you are listening to your body's signals, you will hear them say "enough."

Also, when you begin to develop a respect for your body, you take a step toward respecting yourself. When you focus on the health and emotional benefits of exercise, you are telling yourself that you are worth taking care of.

WHEN MOTIVATION IS A PROBLEM

You know you need to exercise, but you just can't seem to find the time. What can you do?

Schedule It In

When do you enjoy exercising the most? Some people like to start their day with a brief workout, some like a break at noon, others enjoy the stress relief at the end of a long day. Picking a time of day that works for you will help you stick to it and will maximize the psychological benefits.

Also, what is *convenient* for you? When can you make time to do it? Is there a health club close to your home or work, or do you prefer working out at home? Developing a consistent schedule doesn't rule out flexibility; however, if you are committed to exercising on a regular basis, it is important to treat it as seriously as you would any other appointment.

Only Do What You Like

There are arguments for virtually every imaginable form of exercise. There is also no right exercise for everyone. The form of exercise you do should depend on two criteria: (1) Do you like it? and (2) What do you want to accomplish?

I have seen clients who say they get bored after two weeks of the same kind of exercise. That's okay — change it every two weeks. Rather than get into battles with willpower and discipline, why not do a lot of different activities?

Get involved in a team sport. For women in particular, this can be a very rewarding experience. The exercise itself is fun, and the health and emotional benefits are a bonus. Try something new; a friend of mine who recently got involved in yoga is delighted by the body awareness, stretching and control aspects this activity provided her.

In regard to health, different "categories" of exercise will help you accomplish different goals. Aerobic exercise, which includes almost any physical activity that requires consistent movement over time, helps us increase our overall fitness, strengthens our heart muscles and builds up our endurance. Within this category is a myriad of choices — walking, jumping rope, dancing, swimming and so on. The key is to do the activity of your choice for a sustained time period (20 to 60 minutes) without stopping.

To strengthen your muscles, weight training is probably your best bet. Nautilus equipment and free weights are the most popular; lifting more repetitions of a lighter weight helps tone the muscles, while fewer repetitions at higher weights encourages muscle growth. If you are trying to build up muscles, most professionals recommend that you allow at least one day in between workouts. This allows the muscles to recover and helps prevent injury.

WHEN EXCESSIVE EXERCISE IS THE PROBLEM

Maybe your problem is that you just can't seem to *stop* exercising, or even stop *thinking* about your next workout. Here are some tips.

Find Out What's Underneath

If you endorsed three or more of the items in the "At Risk For Overexercise" questionnaire earlier, look at your answers to find clues as to what exercise is "making up for" and how it is affecting your life.

For example, if you answered True to questions linking exercise to the way you feel about your appearance (questions 1, 7, 10 and 14), overexercise may be a way to give a temporary boost to a consistently poor body image. Remember: not only will overexercise do little to change the way you feel about your body, it can actually work against you. The potential appearance benefits, such as increased calorie expenditure and weight maintenance, may go away if you push your body too far.

Do you find yourself using exercise to escape relationship problems or to avoid being alone? Do you spend time thinking about your exercise routine rather than tackling a difficult work project? Once you've identified how exercise is helping you cope with other areas of your life, you can begin to think of other ways to meet those needs.

You may need to cut back on your exercise before you can see clearly how exercise is compensating for other problems. Do this slowly, by substituting another fun activity one day a week in the beginning. If you enjoy the exercise environment, try coaching a sports team or volunteering for your local Special Olympics. There are a lot of ways to enjoy the social aspects of exercise without the physical overload of excessive exercise.

If the fear of potential weight gain is holding you back, it may be helpful to monitor your weight during this period. Weighing yourself once a week will assure you that a decreased workout doesn't automatically result in an increased body size!

Cross-Train

Aerobic exercise, particularly running, is the most physically addictive form of exercise. One reason is the physiological high that comes from the release of endorphins. The good feelings you get from aerobic activity can be habit-forming, and soon you find yourself exercising for longer and longer periods of time and setting stricter and stricter goals. Pretty soon, the pressure to feel good can make you feel bad.

Cross-training — alternating aerobic and strength exercises — can be an effective way to combat the physiological addiction that can come with aerobic exercise. It can also keep you from measuring your exercise success through one exercise, minimizing the risk of the stricter and stricter goal trap. As an added bonus, a combination of strength training and aerobic activity has been found to be the most effective in terms of physical and health benefits.

Synthetic Fitness: Men And Steroid Abuse

As early as 1949, researchers linked exercise to masculinity. A 1951 study concluded that "there is evidence that weightlifting men, compared with those who engage in other athletic activities, are more likely to be compensating for a lowered sense of masculinity."

Times have changed, and the way we view weightlifting has changed too. Many self-assured men lift weights, and studies have found that a moderate program of strength training can enhance feelings of pride and confidence in one's body. Yet for men whose view of their own bodies is significantly different from their ideal body, strength training can begin a downward spiral.

Jimmy is a 28-year-old stockbroker who began strength training at age 14. He was small as a child and felt particularly bad that his sister, one year younger, was larger than he was for much of their childhood. This was the source of much family teasing.

Puberty brought both pluses and minuses. Jimmy was naturally coordinated and developed a strong interest in sports. Coaches told him he looked promising — except for his size. While 5'10" is the average height for American men, it is not the normal height for football players. Jimmy couldn't change his height, but he was determined to change his small frame. He started weight training.

Initially, Jimmy enjoyed lifting weights, and felt stronger and more powerful than ever. However, he quickly became dissatisfied with his progress; it was much slower than he had thought it would be. Also, no matter how hard he pushed, he felt limited by his natural shape. The Atlas look-alikes in the gym didn't help either; they provided a constant and painful source of comparison. When Jimmy was offered steroids by a fellow strength trainer, the choice was easy.

While the expectations and demands of athletic performance have been a longstanding cross for men to bear, the emerging muscle-man beauty ideal has resulted in added pressure. For some men, particularly those who are dissatisfied with their physique, the increasing cultural demands to achieve the muscular build can push them further along the continuum of bodily concern.

As the discrepancy between their "ideal" bodies and their current body perception grows, they may begin ingesting steroids in an effort to achieve a perfectionistically exaggerated musclebound look. While sports performance was the number-one reason cited by 72 current and former steroid abusers, *nearly two-thirds* cited a desire to improve their appearance as another major reason. Teen boys may be particularly prone to use steroids so they don't look like "wimps" or because they believe they will be more attractive to girls. Most were aware of the health risks associated with steroid abuse, yet those risks were generally dismissed or minimized by the study's participants.

Steroid Use: Unclear Gains, Clear Risks

Two to 3 million Americans, most of them men, ingest steroids.* A 1987 study suggests that 250,000 to 500,000 adolescent males do, too. Estimates of steroid use among professional football players, particularly linebackers and linemen, run as high as 50 percent.

---

*Women, however, are not exempt from steroid abuse, especially among the ranks of amateur and professional athletes.

There is considerable controversy about the actual muscle growth benefits associated with steroid use. It appears that steroids do enhance muscle growth and strength temporarily under very specific conditions. The person taking steroids must have a history of strength training prior to taking steroids, be on a high-calorie, high protein diet, and *must continue to train* intensively during the period of steroid use. Even under these conditions, the risk of muscle injury may offset any benefits.

The risks, in the form of dangerous short- and long-term side effects, are much less controversial. While the degree to which steroid use causes some of these diseases is unclear, steroid abuse has clearly been associated with the following side effects:

- short term:
  sleep disturbances
  personality changes (moodiness, increased aggression)
  skin problems
  masculine development in women
  impulsivity
- long term:
  addiction to steroids (due to depression upon withdrawal)
  amphetamine abuse (due to depression upon withdrawal)
  liver damage (including liver tumors)
  high blood pressure
  increased risk of heart disease and stroke
  stunted growth (if started in adolescence)

What To Do About Steroid Abuse

Most people who abuse steroids are aware of the potential health risks and choose to discount them. The short-term benefits, in terms of a muscular appearance and temporary muscle enhancement, can easily cloud the long-term picture. As long as professional athletes are idealized in this culture, and the male beauty ideal includes super-muscles, steroid abuse is likely to continue. In Chapter 10 we will look at ways that we can act to change some of the pressures men and women face in today's society.

Jimmy did not believe he needed help during his period of steroid abuse, nor did he seek it. Only after the fact has he expressed considerable worry and concern over the possibility of long-term health hazards. I do not think Jimmy is unusual in that regard.

My advice with regard to steroid abuse is threefold. First, if you are taking steroids, STOP. Get immediate medical supervision, and realize that short-term withdrawal signs are likely and will go away. Feelings of depression are not uncommon. It is particularly important to get support during this time, as it may be easy to self-medicate (through alcohol or amphetamines) to help you get through this "down" time.

Second, if you are concerned about someone who is taking steroids, TELL HIM. Focus specifically on what you are concerned about, and tell him how his steroid abuse is hurting your relationship with him. For example, if you have noticed an increase in irritability or aggressiveness toward you, give specific examples. It is also important to make sure you are physically safe; you may have to withdraw from the relationship if his behavior becomes erratic.

Third, if you have a history of steroid abuse, get ongoing medical supervision. Make sure your physician is knowledgeable about the long-term risks of steroid use. Getting regular blood pressure and liver enzyme checks can alert you to any arising medical complications. Regular checkups can also give you greater peace of mind.

A Final Thought About Exercise: Moderation And Consistency

Moderate and consistent exercise is associated with stress relief, increased metabolism and decreased health risks. For many of us, exercise has another association — looking good. Yet studies indicate that if looking good is your primary motivator, you are not only less likely to enjoy your exercise, you are less likely to do it consistently. Even if you can discipline yourself into a routine, you are likely to see it as a chore rather than as a self-nurturing activity.

On the other hand, if you find a form of exercise you enjoy, and focus on the pleasure of doing it rather than the possible (looks-related) outcome, exercise can help you appreciate your body in a new way. You will come to appreciate what your body does, not just how it looks.

Exercise and fitness should be a personal choice. Choose the amount and type of exercise you do according to your preferences and your body's comfort signals. No amount of societal approval can make up for feeling out of control and driven to exercise — or for feeling constant guilt if you don't.

Eating and exercise aren't the only avenues for the appearance-obsessed. In the next chapter, we'll look at another socially encouraged activity — clothes shopping.

7

WHEN CLOTHES
HIDE TOO MUCH

Claudia recently asked me if I had ever heard of "binge shopping." While she was laughing at the time, it was obvious that underneath she was worried. When I asked her to explain, here's what she said:

"I've recently realized that I shop when I am stressed. I don't mean window shop, I mean shop to buy. You know how busy I've been at work recently. I could feel the stress inside me building up, and yesterday it exploded. I went to the mall on a lunch break, and in one hour I spent an incredible amount of money.

"Buying new clothes was exhilarating. I had visual images of how great I would look in them. I bought things that I didn't need. I even bought things that aren't really me, you know, thinking I would try a 'new look.' I truly felt out of control. Today I feel guilty and ashamed. I know I can take most of the clothes back if I want to. What really concerns me is that I realize I have done this over and over."

Many articles have been written on compulsive shopping, assessing and analyzing the causes, the motivations and the patterns behind this problem. I have yet to read one that addresses *what we are shopping for* — clothes and beauty products to help us cope with an appearance-obsessed society.

In this chapter, we will look at the pluses and minuses of clothes shopping, and explore what clothes shopping will and won't do for us. We'll also look at what makes some people more at risk for excessive clothes shopping than others. Finally we will explore the motivation behind, and the consequences of, our clothes purchases, and what we can do if we find that our shopping is getting out of control. In short, we will identify and explore that fine line between healthy clothes shopping and shopping to excess.

What Are We Shopping For?

Most women feel pressure to keep up with the latest fashion, wear cosmetics and keep an extensive wardrobe to match a variety of social and business situations. When the styles change with the seasons, and vary from year to year, we are understandably sensitive to the "messages" our clothes send. How often do we feel uncomfortable when someone sees us wearing the same outfit, even if it fits us well or is relatively new? Is it any wonder that 15 million Americans — most of them women — are compulsive spenders?

Because shopping is a socially-encouraged activity there is often a fine line between clothes shopping as a temporary boost of esteem, and a reliance on clothes shopping to meet other needs. Most of us get a psychological boost when we buy a new outfit. Wearing a flattering color or a style that suits our figure can help us temporarily feel better about the way we look. Buying something for ourselves can be a reward at the end of a particularly stressful work week. Shopping can also distract us from our problems, and it can give us a lift when we find ourselves brooding about a dilemma that we are temporarily unable to solve. When we keep these temporary benefits in perspective, shopping can be a healthy and self-nurturing activity.

Yet, like exercise, excessive clothes shopping can also be a way to cope with appearance obsession. Twenty-three percent of my survey respondents said they tended to use fashion to compensate for a negative body image. Relying on clothes to hide our painful body image is not uncommon. If we can't hide our bodies with clothes, we may hide in other ways; more than one of every five female survey respondents said they would avoid a social situation if they didn't have the right outfit.

In light of the conglomeration of women's fashion magazines, it is not surprising that more women (31 percent) reported this coping style than did men (10 percent). Women also spent a higher percentage of their monthly income on clothes purchases. These two findings, in combination, suggest that women may be more at risk for financial difficulties as a result of their spending habits. Nineteen percent of the women said they had experienced shopping-related money problems, while 11 percent of the men agreed that shopping had caused money troubles.

Relying on clothes to make up for a negative body image is at best a temporary fix. As a friend of mine said, "When I buy an expensive dress, the first time I wear it I feel like a million dollars. The next time I wear the same outfit the value seems to depreciate; because it is no longer new it doesn't have the same psychological effect. Pretty soon I find myself going out and buying another expensive outfit."

Shopping can also be used to help us cope with painful feelings. Thirty-four percent of the women said that shopping was a major way to relieve stress; in a 1990 Virginia Slims poll, 60 percent of the women surveyed said they often or sometimes used shopping as stress relief. Occasionally, most women use a new outfit to get rid of the blues, to reduce appearance anxiety in a frightening social situation or to regain a sense of control after a relationship quarrel. Taken to excess, this coping style can leave us feeling out of control, more depressed and overly dependent on social approval. And as we have seen, it can create serious financial difficulties.

Who's At Risk For Excessive Shopping?

Because of the greater emphasis on women's fashion, women tend to shop more than men. Women's beauty care also tends to be more complex and more expensive; consider the array of activities we do to "improve" our appearance — including clothes and

cosmetic purchases, facials, hair and nail appointments and make-
overs. Take these two cultural realities together and we find that
women tend to have more financial troubles as a result of overspending.

However, the extent to which we begin to rely on our shopping
and clothes purchases, and the likelihood that we will encounter
financial difficulties, depends on a number of factors. We are
more likely to rely on shopping and clothes purchases if: (a) we
place a high degree of importance on the way we look; (b) if we
believe that fashionable clothes are an essential ingredient in "looking good"; and (c) if we have doubts about our ability to "look
good" naturally. Sound familiar?

This makes a lot of sense. If we place a high priority on the
way we look, yet don't naturally feel good about our appearance,
we are in a bind. We are likely to feel a considerable amount of
tension between our desire to meet an important goal (to look
good), and the fact that we don't naturally feel that we look good
enough. If clothes become an avenue for closing this gap, one way
to (at least temporarily) reduce this tension is to "buy" a feeling
of looking good. Unfortunately, over time, we also may be buying
a lot of financial concerns (see Figure 7.1.).

Other factors place us at risk for excessive shopping. Researchers have identified the following characteristics that tend
to differentiate people who depend on shopping from people who
are more easily able to put shopping and clothes in perspective.
Put a star by any of the following "at risk" factors that seem to
describe you:

- a family history of addictive behaviors
- low self-esteem (which may make us vulnerable to advertisements
  that link products with improving our image or looks)
- dissatisfaction with looks or body
- family history of love or approval expressed through money or gifts
- difficulty tolerating painful or uncomfortable feelings
- strong need to be liked and get along with others
- frequently feel envious or jealous of others

All of the above factors are positively related to excessive shopping. When we find one, we are more likely to find another. The
more factors that are present, the more at risk we are for a

dependence on shopping. If we have four or more of these risk factors, we need to evaluate the role of shopping in our lives carefully.

Figure 7.1. The Cyclic Nature Of Compulsive Shopping

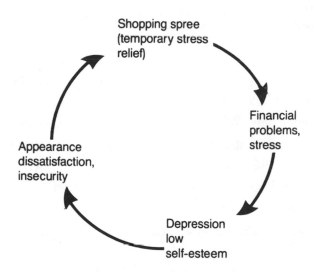

These risk factors often work together. For example, if we have trouble tolerating painful feelings and associate love or approval with purchases, shopping might be a natural coping strategy in response to an upsetting event. If we have a strong need to be liked by others and view clothes as an important statement about ourselves, we may be easily influenced by advertisements or salespeople. The bottom line is that the way we feel about ourselves and our associations with money and spending have a lot to do with how much we will rely on shopping and clothes purchases.

ARE YOUR CLOTHES CONTROLLING YOU?

Answer the following questions to see how much influence your clothes purchases have on you.

Clothes Shopping Dependency Scale

Answer each question with the number that best describes you:

1 = never
2 = rarely
3 = sometimes
4 = often
5 = almost always

1. ____ When I find an outfit that I like in a store, I am unable to leave without buying it.

2. ____ Buying new clothes is a major way to relieve stress.

3. ____ I use fashionable clothes to compensate for the negative view I have of my body.

4. ____ I feel it is extremely important to wear the latest fashion.

5. ____ I have gotten into financial difficulty over my spending habits.

6. ____ I have avoided social situations when I didn't have the "right" outfit to wear.

7. ____ I shop to relieve feelings of boredom, loneliness or depression.

8. ____ My shopping habits have caused significant conflict with others (parents, spouse, boyfriend and so on).

9. ____ I find myself impulsively buying clothes that I don't really need.

10. ____ I feel guilty about the amount of money I spend on clothes.

11. ____ Purchasing clothes is a way I "pay someone back" when they have hurt or angered me ("someone" usually means a significant other or a family member).

12. ____ I hide my clothes purchases from others.

13. ____ When I am stressed, I buy things that aren't really "me."

14. ____ I regret clothes purchases after I have made them.

15. ___ I have a hard time controlling my use of credit cards.

16. ___ I am easily influenced by salespeople.

Scoring: Add up the numbers that correspond to your answers. The total score is your clothes shopping dependency score.

16–41: You do not rely on clothes shopping as a major coping strategy. You are likely to purchase clothes primarily out of need, and tend to think through clothes purchases before you make them.

42–60: Your clothes purchases are sometimes based on emotional rather than material need. It will be helpful for you to complete the pattern analysis that follows to see when and why you may rely on spending or clothes to help you feel more comfortable or secure. Unless you are in financial difficulty or have a relationship conflict concerning money, understanding your areas of vulnerability and expanding your coping options in those situations will be effective.

61–80: Your clothes shopping is an important way you cope with a variety of situations and feelings. It will be helpful for you to complete the pattern analysis that follows, and to assess your pattern of spending. If your spending is creating serious financial difficulties or relationship conflicts, it will be important to build in delays to your spending. If you continue to feel out of control of your shopping after trying some of the balance-building strategies later in this chapter, consult the Resources at the end of the book.

Assessing Why, When And How Much You Shop

A reliance on clothes shopping can take many different forms. You may normally feel in control of your clothes spending, yet, like Claudia, find yourself "binge shopping" in response to upsetting or threatening events. You may buy clothes in response to a relationship breakup or a particularly stressful day at work. You may feel anxious about an upcoming social event and search for the perfect confidence-building outfit. Your credit cards may help you feel back in control. Or you may simply bask in the temporary boost you feel about your looks.

Fashion may have become your hobby — you shop daily or several times a week. For you, shopping may initially be an adventure in pursuit of the latest fashion trend or a routine reward at the end of a workday. However, if you find that you are unable to do without it, your hobby may have become your habit.

Another pattern of clothes shopping that can get you into trouble is multiple buying. You initially assess your wardrobe needs and go shopping with the intent to fill them. Yet, when you get to the store, you find yourself buying several items. You find the one pair of shoes that you were looking for and come home with six additional pairs. The pleasure and the power of spending overcomes you, and only when you get home do you realize that this short-lived pleasure may have long-term consequences.

Whether you overspend in response to emotional pain, lose control of your pocketbook once you get to the store or shop on a daily basis, the underlying motive is often the same. You may be looking for the *feeling* that shopping (or buying) gives you more than the outcome. You may be seeking the attention that you can easily get from salespeople, the power and control of being the decision-maker or the reassurance that your attractive outfit can hide a negative body image.

Of course, with our society's preoccupation with beauty, the power of spending and the advantages of fashionable clothes purchases can easily become intertwined. Gloria Steinem once said that women have traditionally held two sources of power — beauty/sexuality and shopping. What better way to combine the two than clothes shopping?

Regardless of the unquestionable approval clothes shopping brings, we alone are the ones who experience the consequences. Earlier in the chapter we saw how, depending on our personal histories, some of us may be more at risk for a reliance on clothes shopping than others. Completing the clothes shopping dependency scale gave you some indication of how much you are currently relying on clothes purchases. The next step is to assess *how* you are relying on clothes shopping and the degree to which this is causing you personal and financial difficulties.

Look back at your answers to the Clothes Shopping Dependency Scale. If you answered "often" or "almost always" to the following questions, it may be important for you to balance clothes shopping with additional ways of handling these problem areas.

For questions 3, 4 and 6: You may be relying on clothes to compensate for a painful relationship with your appearance. Situations that trigger anxiety about your looks are likely to result in clothes shopping. In addition, a chronically negative body image may result in a regular reliance on clothes to make up for your appearance dissatisfaction.

For questions 2, 7, 9 and 14: Clothes shopping may be a way to cope with painful feelings. In particular, stress may trigger a shopping response.

For questions 8, 12 and 13: Your clothes shopping may be directly related to relationship conflict. Whether your clothes shopping precipitated the conflict, or whether your shopping is due to relationship struggles about money, your responses indicate that your shopping may be tied to anger at a significant other.

For questions 1, 5, 10, 11, 15 and 16: These questions provide information about the impact of your shopping. Regardless of the reasons behind your clothes shopping, if you endorsed several of these items, you are likely to be experiencing considerable emotional turmoil about your shopping. You also may be at high risk for serious financial difficulties. It is imperative that you initially focus on behavior change.

BALANCING YOUR CLOTHES AND BEAUTY SHOPPING

Let's look at some of the strategies you can use to keep your shopping trips in balance.

Build In Delays

If you find that you tend to be an impulsive clothes purchaser, build in delays to your spending. Leave that outfit in the store and give yourself the option to purchase it later. Most stores will hold an outfit for a few hours. By giving yourself time to think through your purchase, it will help you evaluate whether or not to make the purchase more objectively. Leave the price tags on your purchases when you get home — and give yourself a few days before you wear them. Both of these delay strategies will give you time to assess the possible financial and emotional consequences.

Budget Is Not A Four-Letter Word

While many of us cringe at the mere sound of the word "budget," setting aside a clothes allowance will reassure you that some clothes purchases are allowed. If necessary, put your clothes allowance in a separate account. When you go shopping, leave your credit cards at home. It can also be helpful to give yourself a small amount of flexibility so that your purchasing guidelines don't feel too restrictive.

Separate Your Feelings From Your Wallet

Buying a new outfit when you're down in the dumps can give you an emotional lift. This is especially true when you have several other options for handling the blues, and only use clothes shopping occasionally. Problems arise, however, when the ways you distract yourself from your feelings keep you from dealing with them.

Separating your feelings from your wallet first involves identifying what these feelings are. Feelings are our most valuable sources of information; they let us know when something is wrong. They let us know what emotional needs are not being met.

If you feel lonely, for instance, this is information that your need for companionship is not being met. Identifying this feeling and the underlying need gives you the opportunity to take action. You can respond by increasing your social interactions or you may use this information to build intimacy in your current relationships. If you distract yourself through shopping, you may hide your loneliness from yourself temporarily but the underlying problem is never addressed.

Build Your Body Image

Chapter 10 looks at some specific strategies that you can use to build your body image. If you find that a reliance on clothes shopping is linked to your negative view of your body, work on the two together. It is hard to give up a comfortable coping strategy if the underlying pain remains. Building a firm foundation of appearance security while you are modifying your clothes shopping can help you replace a security blanket with lasting security.

Continued Debt Signals The Need For Help

It is very important to take a sense of desperation over shopping or continued debt very seriously. Like any addiction, compulsive shopping can have devastating personal consequences if it goes untreated. If you are unable to build in delays to your shopping or are in serious financial difficulties, it is time to seek professional help. Consult the Resources at the end of this book to get support with the problem.

Clothes And Relationships

Clothes shopping can involve relationship issues. Ashamed of our reliance on clothes purchases, yet hooked on the good feeling that shopping gives us, we may hide our spending habits from our partners. Or being afraid to express our anger directly, we may retaliate with spending. Regardless of the specific dynamics, our appearance insecurities can easily turn into relationship battles concerning money.

My friend Mary painfully told me about her past struggles to balance her reliance on clothes with the turmoil this caused in her relationship with her husband. Mary had always been very looks-conscious and took pride in being a sharp dresser. Her clothes purchases frequently squeezed her budget, yet somehow she managed to keep her head above water. The financial stress she felt seemed less important than the temporary sense of confidence her clothes purchases provided.

When she met her husband, Tim, he frequently complimented her on her fashion sense. Mary still believes that her "together" appearance was a big attraction for her husband when they first met, yet noted that he had no idea how much money her extensive wardrobe and meticulous appearance was costing her. After they were married, her spending habits did not change. What did change was the impact her spending had on their relationship.

Mary and her husband made the same amount of money, but they sometimes had different ideas about how it should be spent. When they bought a house, for instance, Tim wanted to spend a considerable amount of money redecorating it — his money and her money. Mary also wanted to invest in the new house, yet she also wanted to maintain her wardrobe budget. She felt ashamed and guilty over the priority she gave to her clothes, and was uncomfortable talking about this with him. Mary also believed that her husband wanted her to continue to look good but didn't understand the financial resources this required.

Over time their arguments about money escalated. Mary found herself heading for the mall after every money-related quarrel. She also found herself hiding her clothes purchases and becoming increasingly skilled at finding ways to keep her shopping from her husband. While this temporarily reduced the outright conflict in their relationship, Mary increasingly felt like a rebellious daughter rather than a wife. Their relationship continued to suffer.

Clearly, Mary and Tim's relationship issues about money needed to be addressed in the relationship rather than outside of it. As long as Mary reacted to their financial conflict by spending more, the less their chances were of reaching an acceptable compromise. The more Tim focused on and tried to control Mary's clothes purchases, the further apart they grew.

Hiding her purchases gave Mary a temporary sense of financial freedom, yet she also felt ashamed and guilty over her behavior. Her guilt often led to more anger and frustration toward Tim, and when Tim discovered Mary's deception, his anger also increased.

Eventually, Mary and Tim were able to resolve their situation. They first agreed to analyze their individual incomes and to clearly establish their financial goals and priorities. They each established a personal budget, with the agreement that they would subsequently get together and negotiate a family one. Part of their individual analyses involved establishing a time frame for their house redecorating and establishing "must haves" and "can do withouts" regarding hobbies and personal spending.

While Tim was struggling with his own conflicts concerning money, Mary spent time assessing her personal feelings about her appearance and worked hard to feel more secure about her looks. Instead of beating herself up for her reliance on clothes shopping, she evaluated her salary and included in her budget a modified clothes allowance. Being clear about her own goals and desires increased Mary's sense of personal power. It also helped her identify underlying appearance insecurities and strengthened her desire to build a better body image. Finally, after a series of family budget negotiations, they reached a successful compromise. In addition, Tim gained a new appreciation of how much appearance maintenance can cost!

A Final Thought About Clothes Shopping

When do clothes hide too much? When we depend on our clothes to hide a negative body image. When we consistently manage our stress through out-of-control shopping. When we would miss out on a fun social situation rather than risk wearing the "wrong" outfit.

In each of these instances, we are relying on something on the outside to make up for something that's missing on the inside. While this coping strategy may distract us from our problems effectively, it does not solve them. In addition, if taken to extremes, it can create serious financial difficulties.

We have also seen how a reliance on shopping can have a negative effect on our relationship with others and can lead to control battles concerning money. Appearance obsession affects our relationships in many other ways. Turn to the next chapter to see what they are — and what we can do about them.

WILL YOU
BE MY MIRROR?

Female Bodybuilder Wanted. Single, white male who is into working out every day seeks female workout partner for friendship and possible relationship. Only females who are into working out or weightlifting need call.

Dallas Observer Romance Classifieds, May 6-13, 1993

Appearance obsession is a personal struggle, yet we have already seen some examples of how it can indirectly interfere with our relationships. The hunger pangs of dieting, and the low energy level and the sense of deprivation that go with them, can leave us with a short fuse which can easily turn into a family dispute. Excessive exercise cuts into the amount of time we have to spend with others and can be used as a way to avoid intimacy. An overdependence on spending can lead to relationship conflicts about money.

Appearance obsession can also affect our relationships in direct ways. We may compare our looks to others and feel either envious or dejected by the outcome. We may be very sensitive to appearance comments from others; with our looks and identity so closely tied together, why wouldn't we be? We may rely on attractive dates for confirmation of our own attractiveness. Or, if we notice our date or spouse eyeing an attractive individual, we may respond with jealousy and insecurity.

All of these painful emotions take a tremendous amount of energy. In addition, they can be confusing. Am I feeling this way because of my relationship, or is it a personal problem? Are you untrustworthy, or am I so scared of rejection or disapproval that I am unwilling to risk being open and honest? How much of this is me and how much of this is you?

Because our cultural beauty messages are so pervasive, we can see (and feel) appearance pressures everywhere. Personal concerns can easily turn into relationship issues. For instance, we may already believe that looking good is a necessary part of the dating scene; comments from a romantic partner turn into evidence that confirms this belief. We may bond with same-sex friends over appearance concerns, yet feel an underlying push to compete with them. Or we may hide our weaknesses and fears from others, seeking confirmation for our own lack of self-worth. In each of these instances, appearance obsession has a negative impact on our relationships. This chapter will help you sort these out.

Acting Or Interacting: The Need For Approval

When we are painfully unsure of ourselves and chronically dissatisfied with our appearance, we may find ourselves focusing on how we are appearing to others rather than risk being ourselves. We direct our efforts toward creating a positive impression, hoping this will make up for our low feelings about ourselves. We never go out in public without looking our best, we check our appearance frequently and we worry about what others think of us. We rely on the approval of others to determine our own self-worth. Maybe if someone else believes we are confident in who we are and likes how we look, we will too.

During a conversation, we may catch ourselves wondering what the other person is thinking of us rather than hearing what he or she has to say. It's as if we are outside of ourselves, constantly watching and critiquing our "performance." We tune in to the expectations or cues that we pick up from others, or we change our behavior to match a situation. We may even plan and rehearse how we will act in advance to ensure that we make the "right" impression. Over time this focus on managing our public self, the part that others see, can lower our sensitivity and awareness of our private self, our inner thoughts and feelings.

Some of us may go to greater lengths than others to create a positive impression. Three factors determine the extent of our motivation to impress others. First, it is determined by how much the opinions of others directly influence our self-worth. Second, if we place a high value on the outcome of a social interaction, we are obviously more motivated to try to make sure the other person sees us in a positive light. And, third, if there is a discrepancy between how we see ourselves and how we would like to be seen, we may try to compensate for this discrepancy by making our outside self look like our ideal self. Together, these three set the stage for *impression management.*

Some of our impression-management strategies may center on our looks, others may not. In college I had friends who would eat before they went on a date so they could eat lightly while they were out. Some studies suggest that most women will eat less in front of an attractive man than when they are with a female friend. Certainly almost all of the women I know will eat more when they are alone than when they are with someone else.

We might argue that the above example is a relatively harmless one. After all, we can always grab something to eat later. We are likely to eat more "honestly" as the relationship progresses. Isn't putting our best foot forward the usual way we start out in relationships?

I have different questions. Why should putting our best foot forward have anything to do with food? Why should our eating habits change depending on who we are with? Our body's need for nourishment doesn't! Because our society links dieting to self-control, thinness to success and eating "like a bird" with femininity, the amount we eat and the food choices we make can feel like a statement about ourselves.

A BARRIER TO INTIMACY: GETTING TRAPPED BY OUR ROLES

Just as we may be stuck in a vicious cycle of self-improvement, we may also feel stuck in our need to control the image we present. When our need for approval becomes too important, we may end up feeling lonely and alone no matter who we are with. When we are unsure of our own self-worth, we are not about to risk having our worst fears confirmed by someone else. Instead, we hide our fears and weaknesses and give to others what we think they expect or want.

Melinda's story provides some insight into how our appearance obsession can prevent intimacy. As a 27-year-old marketing executive, Melinda firmly believes that "looking good" is a critical part of today's singles scene. In addition to her demanding job, she spends a large portion of her spare time on looks-related activities. She gets her nails done weekly, her hair colored monthly and she exercises religiously. She puts on makeup (even if she's just running to the grocery store), keeps up with the latest fashions and keeps tight control over her food intake.

When she is with her boyfriend she often finds herself "checking out the competition," and feels jealous if he pays attention to another woman. Of course, she would never let him know this. She copes with these feelings either by evening the score (talking to an attractive man) or by working harder to get her boyfriend's attention. When she feels jealous, Melinda alternates between directing her anger at her "rival" and at herself.

Melinda's friends are very much like she is. Many of them have had plastic surgery, and all of them diet, exercise and keep up with the latest fashions. Melinda is very aware of this. While she and her friends often share their self-improvement strategies, there is an underlying air of competition and comparison. She often looks at her friends for evidence of how *she* is faring on the appearance scale. She secretly prizes her figure over her heavier friends, and feels threatened by friends who are slimmer or more attractive than she views herself.

Melinda is aware of the underlying competition that characterizes her friendships with other women. She also acknowledges that her own competitive edge often prevents her from sharing her disappointments, insecurities or fears with her friends, partic-

ularly about her looks. She feels trapped by her appearance obsession, but is afraid to give up the facade of having it all together.

Melinda's concern about her social presentation affects her intimacy with others in other areas. For example, during a recent
period of extreme job turmoil, Melinda did not tell her best friend
until she felt in control of her painful feelings. Her fear about
imagined criticism overshadowed her ability to reach out for emotional support. In this situation, Melinda gave more power to her
friend's approval than to herself.

Short-Term Rewards, Long-Term Loneliness

In the short term, investing our energy in how we present
ourselves can work. Over the long haul, however, several drawbacks appear. First, like Melinda, we may miss out on much-
needed emotional support. I have seen eating-disordered clients
who, out of their personal shame and fear of rejection, hid daily
binging and purging from significant others *for years.*

Second, when we continually focus on the expectations and
desires of others, we may eventually feel confused about who we
are. The roles we adopt become so familiar that the underlying
actor or actress is lost.

Finally, while we may be able to get acceptance and approval
from others and reduce the risk of rejection by pretending to be
the person we want to be rather than who we are, the approval
or acceptance of others means nothing to our self-esteem. After
all, they aren't seeing the *real* us. This can perpetuate our underlying belief that our *real self* is unacceptable, and lead us to rely
even more on our image or our impression.

Feeling trapped in a role, hiding our true feelings from others
and changing our behavior to fit the person we are with are all
signs that our appearance obsession may be limiting us. Unfortunately, some of these feelings are fairly common. Here's what my
survey respondents said:

I frequently feel trapped in a certain role.

- 30 percent of the women said yes
- 19 percent of the men said yes

I act dramatically different depending on who I am with.

- 22 percent of the women said yes
- 26 percent of the men said yes

The way I appear to others is frequently not the way I am really feeling.

- 45 percent of the women said yes
- 36 percent of the men said yes

There is definitely an appearance connection. In fact, a high degree of sensitivity to and reliance on social approval was the strongest predictor of appearance obsession. For both men and women, the more dissatisfied they were with their appearances, the more likely they were to answer yes to these questions.

Appearance obsession blocks our intimacy with others by reducing our willingness to be open and honest with others. Understanding our fears about opening up and exploring where these fears came from is a first step toward intimacy. However, the bottom line is risk. Taking small steps and reassuring ourselves about our ability to handle the consequences of our involvement with others can promote our behavior change. The benefits of risk are obvious; we increase our satisfaction with our relationships, and we increase our self-esteem and build our confidence. In addition, changing our behavior will provide information not only about ourselves but about the people in our lives. Let's look at some strategies for change.

SOLUTIONS

To Know Yourself Is To Like Yourself

When you are unsure of who you are, you are more likely to rely on feedback from others for clues about yourself. You also may rely on interpersonal strategies, such as impressing others, as a means of developing a clear sense of who you are. These strategies are understandable, yet they make you vulnerable to your surroundings.

Getting to know yourself is the best step you can take to reduce your need for social approval. In fact, some studies indicate that a low self-esteem may partly reflect a lack of self-knowledge.

When you get to know yourself — your values, goals, thoughts and feelings — you give yourself a firm foundation for handling changing or challenging events.

How can you get to know yourself? One way is to dedicate ten minutes a day to keeping a journal. Another way is to learn to meditate — to spend one evening alone each week, with the TV and radio off, getting in touch with your inner thoughts and feelings. You may want to develop a personal mission statement. In his book *The Seven Habits of Highly Effective People*, Steven Covey gives very specific advice on how to do this. The method you choose is much less important than your commitment to self-exploration.

Risking Intimacy

Self-disclosure can be alarming because you just don't know how the other person will respond. However, you can make self-disclosure a little easier.

First, realize that the response of the other person is information about him or her, not about you. Second, adopt a "tit-for-tat" approach. Reveal a little bit of information about yourself and see if the other person reciprocates.

If they do, or if they respond in a positive or supportive way, you are initiating a new level of closeness with a friend or significant other. If they don't, you can back off; over time you can evaluate whether this is a person you want to be intimate with. Your willingness to take gradual risks through self-disclosure has much more to do with yourself than with the other person. A willingness to take risks gives you the option to be intimate with others — and who doesn't like having more options?

Social Anxiety

We've already seen how a reliance on the approval of others can reduce our willingness to be ourselves. Another factor also comes into play: a lack of confidence in social situations. A combination of the two is a double whammy; if others are important to us, yet we aren't confident in our ability to relate to others, we are likely to be highly self-conscious in social situations. During social interactions, our need for approval may turn into a *fear of disapproval*.

And how can we minimize this possibility? By adopting a protective strategy: listening rather than sharing personal information, agreeing rather than voicing our opinions and spending our time wondering about how others are perceiving us.

Answer the following questions to see how comfortable you really feel when you are relating to others. This will give you a measure of your *social esteem*, the degree to which you are confident in your social interactions. Research indicates that the less confident you are in social situations, the more at risk you may be for appearance insecurities.

How High Is Your Social Esteem?

Answer each question with one of the following letters:

A = never
B = rarely
C = sometimes
D = often
E = almost always

1. ____ When I meet someone new, I am confident that I will make a good impression.

2. ____ I have a couple of drinks to help me relax before a social situation.

3. ____ It is easy for me to make casual social conversation.

4. ____ I enjoy parties and social gatherings.

5. ____ I rehearse what I will say or do before I meet someone new or when I am on a date.

6. ____ I feel confident in interacting with the opposite sex.

7. ____ When I am talking to someone, I find myself wondering what the other person is thinking of me.

8. ____ I would describe myself as a basically shy person.

9. ____ I will avoid situations if I think a lot of attractive people will be there.

10. ____ In public, I go along with the opinions and choices of others even if I privately don't agree.

11. _____ Other peoples' opinions of me are very important.

Scoring system: For questions 1, 3, 5 and 9, give yourself one point if you answered A, two points if you answered B, three points if you answered C, four points if you answered D and five points if you anwered E.

For questions 2, 4, 6, 7, 8, 10 and 11, give yourself five points if you answered A, four points if you answered B, three points if you answered C, two points if you answered D and one point if you answered E.

Add up your total points to assess your current social esteem.

44–55: You are confident of your abilities in social situations. You are likely to approach social situations with interest and enthusiasm, and you generally have faith in your ability to make a good impression on others.

26–43: Your confidence in social situations fluctuates from time to time. Some social situations may be more comfortable for you than others. It will be helpful to assess your pattern of responses to see what situations may create anxiety for you. Use the tips later on to boost your social esteem so you can make the most of *any* social event.

11–25: Social situations are often frightening for you. You may avoid situations that are extremely uncomfortable. In addition, your anxiety may lead you to adopt a self-protective strategy in your interactions with others — you closely monitor what you say to others and minimize the chances of rejection. While this may reduce your tension, it may also reduce your enjoyment at social events. Use the tips below to help you boost your social esteem.

RAISING YOUR SOCIAL ESTEEM

Lets look at some strategies you can use to raise your social esteem.

Change Your Dress Rehearsal

If you often feel anxious before a social event, develop an action plan that will take your mind off yourself. Rather than worrying about what might happen, or practicing what you will do and say, determine how you can benefit from the event. Make a pact with yourself to meet three new people; or if you are more comfortable one-on-one, determine to really get to know one other person at the party. Having these concrete plans can give you something to do when you first get there, the time when you are likely to feel the most anxious. It will also help you take the pressure off your performance, and help you see what others have to offer you rather than how you are impressing them.

Build Your Skills — And Practice Them

You may feel uncomfortable at parties or feel shy when you meet someone new. You may be able to hide it from others, but underneath you feel tense and anxious. You wonder if the other person can sense your anxiety, which creates even more tension and self-consciousness.

Social skills are just that — *skills*. They are a set of behaviors that can be learned and improved on with practice. I came from a shy family that did not entertain often, and for many years I was uncomfortable at parties. Casual conversation did not come easily to me. After all, I was used to talking about problems with my clients or sharing intimate details with my close friends, topics that are not necessarily the best ice-breakers!

How did I gradually come to feel more confident? I began viewing social events as an opportunity to learn. I watched other people and began to incorporate their behaviors into my own repertoire. Also, as I felt more secure with myself in general, I came to accept and value the fact that I am more of a one-on-one person. It's nice, however, to have the ability to approach social events with ease. By practicing your social skills and working to reduce your anxiety, you can expand your options and get the most from new situations.

The No-Win Comparison Game

Comparing our looks to others is a normal outcome of our society's emphasis on physical appearance. In my survey, 57 percent of the women stated they frequently compared their looks to others; 43 percent of the men did also. The problem arises when this comparison serves to fuel our dissatisfaction with our own appearance or prevents us from being honest and open with others. It occurs when we compare our inside insecurities or doubts about our looks to the outside appearance of others, or when we come to rely on winning a looks comparison contest in order to feel good temporarily about the way we look. It hurts us when we would rather miss out on a fun social situation than run the risk of social comparison.

LESS SATISFACTION WITH OURSELVES, MORE COMPARISON WITH OTHERS

There is a relationship between looks satisfaction and social comparison. The more we compare our looks to others, the more dissatisfied we are likely to be with our appearance. Or the more dissatisfied with our appearance, the more likely we are to seek confirmation from others. Either way, we lose.

How do comparisons with others affect our feelings about our own looks? Won't we boost our appearance satisfaction if we can compare ourselves to someone who is less attractive? Let's look at the research.

First of all, there are two directions we can use when we compare ourselves to others. We can compare ourselves to people who are more attractive than we think we are (an upward comparison), or we can compare ourselves to less attractive individuals (a downward comparison). In general, upward comparisons tend to decrease our satisfaction with our appearance.

Upward comparisons don't tend to alter our opinions of our appearance, they just make us less satisfied with them. Remember my elevator story in Chapter 1? While my looks didn't change with the appearance of a gorgeous woman, my perception of them did. This is usually what happens. If we give ourselves a five on the appearance scale, we will still give ourselves a five in the presence of a ten. However, suddenly a five isn't good enough.

Downward comparisons are not what they may seem to be at first. When we compare ourselves to someone who is less attractive than we think we are, we may get temporary reassurance. With an underlying sense of guilt and shame, we may find ourselves thinking, "At least I don't look like that." Why shouldn't we feel that way when we find ourselves on the losing end of the comparison game so often?

The trap with downward comparisons is twofold. First, when we rely on downward comparisons to boost our appearance esteem, we are likely to assume that others do the same. This is likely to make our sense of discomfort worse when we are around highly attractive people or are in frightening social situations. Second, we are relying on outside influences to make us feel good about ourselves. Sure, we might get a temporary boost when we "win" a comparison. How will we feel the next time a Cindy Crawford look-alike is standing next to us at the gym (see Figure 8.2.)?

SOLUTIONS

Give Your "Looks Talk" A Different Focus

Women, in particular, often bond around dieting and exercise. We compare the results of our latest diets, we share fashion updates, we moan together over the difficulty of our aerobics class. Stuck in our appearance obsession together, many of us at least try to empathize with each other, console each other and support each other. And this is certainly better than overt and direct competition with each other.

But what if we channeled our bonding conversations into problem-solving exercises? Let's begin to talk about the pain and insecurities we feel, our fatigue over all the effort, our fear of giving it up. Let's agree to support each other in *not dieting*, in balancing our exercise routine, in feeling good about the way we look regardless of makeup or a new outfit. The same energy we spend helping each other self-improve can help each of us self-accept.

Directly Address Competition

The more open we can be with each other about our competition, the less likely these feelings are to affect our behavior and ultimately our friendship. Discussing feelings of jealousy or competition is often taboo around friends; yet the longer they linger unaddressed, the more insidious they can become.

Also, the outcome may surprise you. As we saw in Chapter 2, while you may be envying your friend's flat stomach, she may be painfully focused on your slimmer thighs.

What We See Is What We Get

The comparison game is a no-win situation for another reason. Social psychologists have found that two internal variables

Figure 8.2. The Comparison Trap

Upward comparison
— appearance dissatisfaction
— envy
— depression

Downward comparison
— temporary self-esteem boost
— self-consciousness in social
  situations
— dependence on external
  sources for confirmation of
  attractiveness

directly impact the outcome of comparisons — the degree of control that we have over the feature we are comparing and our level of self-esteem.

For example, if we are comparing someone else's job performance to ours, and we believe that we have control over our own effort and success, we have the potential to benefit from this in two ways. We could look for a highly successful person and attempt to learn from him or her, thus providing a role model. In this situation, an upward comparison can be helpful. Even a downward comparison can serve to affirm the good job that we are doing, to reinforce the effort and energy we are putting into our work.

Compare this to the body parts review with which most women are painfully familiar. You know, comparing that one body part that you hate the most with that same body part of every woman you meet. We can all appreciate the sense of failure when we don't measure up, and many women say that a downward comparison often serves as a reminder of what they could look like if they "let themselves go."

Self-esteem comes into play because the way we see ourselves colors the way we see and interpret everything else. Even though the outcome is likely to be painful, when we feel badly about the way we look, we are more likely to attend to things in our environment that confirm our negative view of ourselves. Or we are likely to interpret potential positives in a self-critical way.

How does this work in terms of appearance obsession? We don't believe the compliments we get. Rather than accept that someone else thinks we look good, a little voice inside our head immediately discounts it. Or we hear a compliment as a performance demand; we interpret the compliment as a message for us to keep up our self-improvement regime.

SOLUTION

In Chapter 10, we will look at some specific strategies we can use to boost our body image. For now, work on outwardly accepting compliments from others. Even if you have trouble believing them, say "thank you" — and stop. Don't respond by putting yourself down! Also, remember that compliments let you know how someone else feels; they are not messages about what we should do.

Jealousy And Envy: Comparing Limits Us

Comparing our looks to others takes an inner dilemma and puts it on the outside. A personal problem gets played out in our interactions with others, and, not surprisingly, the way we feel toward others and how we relate to them is changed. Feelings of jealousy and envy are common concerning looks, and they offer us the opportunity to learn about ourselves.

Envy and jealousy are very different emotions. We are most likely to feel envious when we *believe* that someone is, in some way, superior to us. Jealousy involves a relationship threat; when we believe that another person's advantage might interfere with a close relationship, jealousy is a natural response. While these two emotions are often triggered by different situations, they invariably have one thing in common: *these feelings occur when we have compared ourselves to someone and lost.* We are the judge, and we have given the prize to someone else.

This does not mean that others do not sometimes play a part in our feelings. Yet think for a minute. We aren't envious of our friends' success in every area. We can often bask in the rewards of others who are close to us, or we can genuinely admire the accomplishments of people we don't know. It is only when the area of success is one that is important to *us*, one that has a large influence on how we rate *ourselves*, that uncomfortable emotions surface. And the larger the distance between our desired success and our perceived success, the more we are at risk for envy. In a study of more than 5,000 men and women, physical attractiveness was both the number one self-evaluator and inspired the highest level of jealousy and envy.

As most of us know, envy and jealousy often inspire coping behaviors. Like Melinda, we may retaliate in an attempt to regain control or to protect our self-esteem. We may find ourselves making derogatory comments about the source of our envy and jealousy. It may also prevent us from getting to know a potential friend. For instance, 24 percent of the women surveyed stated that they frequently feel threatened by attractive members of the same sex. This makes sense if the looks of others are linked to our own appearance satisfaction. Studies indicate that this threat is most evident between strangers and decreases with friends. If our personal threat is great enough, however, we may feel so uncomfortable that we avoid an attractive person rather than get to know him or her.

SOLUTIONS

Redirect Feelings Of Envy

If you find it hard to be true to who or what you are, you may find yourself envying people who don't. Acknowledging feelings of envy by bringing them to the surface can help you find your own areas of low self-esteem. It can also help you recognize and change your self-defeating beliefs.

Do you find yourself:

- focusing on what others around you have, but what you lack?
- believing that if someone is more attractive, this means you are *not* attractive?
- comparing the outside of others — how they *look* — to how you *feel* on the inside?

If so, the key is to take the focus off the other person and look at unfulfilled areas of your own life. Sources of envy are clues that you aren't satisfied with certain parts of your life. For instance, if you find yourself envying another person's job success, you need to take a close look at your own job satisfaction and, if necessary, find ways to improve it. Problem-solve ways to fill these areas rather than focus on factors over which you have no control.

Understand Your Jealousy

You can make yourself jealous or a significant other can create jealous situations. If you find yourself in a perpetual state of jealousy in your current romantic relationship, here are some questions that will help you determine the best course of action:

- Did you feel this way six months ago? If not, what has changed?
- What specific behaviors are triggering your jealousy?
- Is fidelity a part of your relationship contract? If so, is your partner actively destroying it?

- Do you have a history of intense jealousy or insecurity in relationships?
- Do you find yourself needing more reassurance than any one partner can give?
- Is your jealousy based on concrete information, or is it the result of internal fantasies or fears of betrayal?
- Were either of your parents unfaithful to each other?

If you have a history of jealousy, or you realize your current feelings are based on inner fears rather than concrete evidence, working on your self-esteem is the first step. This doesn't mean that your current relationship isn't contributing; if you are insecure about yourself, you may unconsciously get involved with romantic partners who exacerbate these self-concerns. However, feeling better about yourself first will help you sort this out.

On the other hand, if you have firm pieces of information that your partner is unfaithful, this is a relationship issue. It is also information about your *partner*, not about you. Because this behavior is about your partner rather than you, your influence lies in your communication and your response. Working harder to "win" his or her love will not work. It also sends a message to yourself that you are giving your relationship priority over your self-respect. Directly confronting your partner by focusing on the behavior, how you feel about it and what you want is the best strategy. After that the ball is in your partner's court, while your self-worth remains in yours.

Look Past The Appearance Of Others

We've already seen that as we become friends with someone, looks become much less important. One of my clients, Kathy, recently related a strategy that worked for her. When she and her husband began socializing with another couple, Kathy felt very threatened by the new wife of her husband's friend. This woman was very attractive and spent a considerable amount of time and energy emphasizing her looks. To Kathy, this woman's figure was a ten and hers was a five, on good days.

Kathy initially tried a number of strategies. At first she found herself agonizing over her dress whenever they were going out with this couple. No matter what she wore, Kathy ended up feeling bad. Next she tried the opposite approach; ashamed of her envy and insecurity, she made a pact with herself to stop competing and to wear clothes that were comfortable for her no matter what she imagined the other woman was going to wear. This strategy worked for a short while, yet Kathy found herself secretly making critical and disparaging comments about her new social acquaintance. She began making excuses to avoid getting together with this couple, a plan that resulted in conflict with her spouse. Her husband had no idea why Kathy was avoiding getting together with his friends, and she was too embarrassed to tell him. She also didn't want him to notice how much less attractive *she thought* she was.

When we discussed the possibility that Kathy's new acquaintance might be battling her own appearance obsession, an idea that Kathy had not considered, she began to look at this person in a new way. More importantly, she decided to get to know this woman better, and then to make a decision about future social contact. In the past Kathy's uncertainty about her own attractiveness, which was exacerbated when she was around this woman, had consumed so much energy that she had little left over to really get to know someone else. When she focused on her new acquaintance, she found that they had a lot in common — including a struggle with self-improvement and appearance security.

Men And Women: Clearing Up The Confusion About Looks

During a recent talk, one of the men in my audience said, "I don't understand why women are offended by advertisements that include women in bikinis. I don't mind seeing pictures of men in bathing suits." The majority of the women in the room rolled their eyes and grimaced, their nonverbal gestures signaling a mutual opinion that sometimes men *just don't get it.*

Not only are women more sensitive to, and offended by, the use of sex as advertising, we are more sensitive to comments about our own looks. Forty percent of the women in my study either agreed or strongly agreed with the statement, "I am very sensitive to comments about the way I look." Given the tremendous beauty pressure we face, and the unobtainable beauty ideals that are ready-made measures of comparison, we have good reason to be.

How are men faring on the looks-sensitivity scale? Twenty-three percent of the men in my survey had similar feelings about the impact of feedback from others about looks. An additional 20 percent somewhat agreed with this statement. While I believe we are seeing a gradual meeting in the middle between men and women in terms of appearance pressures, the current discrepancy between male and female sensitivity concerning looks can set the stage for a relationship battleground.

Many of us feel that if we gave up our appearance obsession, we would quickly be rejected by members of the opposite sex. Or we may believe that much of our appearance obsession arises from the pressure and competition we get from same-sex friends. We do get messages from others about the importance of looking good. Men do tend to like slim women, and to the extent that we don't feel slim enough or aren't slim enough, there is a real social basis for attempts at dieting or self-improvement.

Pam, a large-sized 34-year-old, talks with a combination of anger and sadness about the different reactions she gets from men at different weights. A yo-yo dieter for many years, Pam has gone through a variety of body sizes. She has also noticed that the attention she draws from men is related to her body size; the slimmer she is, the more romantic interest she inspires. Men who are overweight, unusually short or who believe they are unattractive have told me similar and equally painful stories.

There is no question that both men and women are influenced by our society's beauty messages, but perhaps not to the extent that we internalize them for ourselves. In fact, when we look at the realities of what men and women like, we find that there is considerable confusion. Here's what the research reveals about appearance pressures from others:

1. Women give a lower attractiveness rating to other females than men do.
2. Women tend to think their female friends prefer a slimmer body shape than is actually true.
3. Men think their peers value a larger, more muscular build than they do.

4. In general, men tend to like larger chests (for themselves) and larger breasts (for women) than women do.
5. Women tend to prefer an even thinner figure than they think men find attractive.
6. Women are more critical of specific body parts than men. In evaluating female figures, men tend to take a more global approach and are less likely to focus on one part of a woman's figure than a woman is.
7. Both women and men rate older women as less attractive. Young men tend to see their own attractiveness as decreasing with age, while women do not tend to see older men as less attractive.

These findings suggest that, yes, just as we thought, there is very real pressure to look good in our society. They suggest that men, women and the media may all play a part in perpetuating the "looks focus" of our society. They also suggest that, at least in part, the judgment or evaluation we see in the eyes of others may sometimes be a mirror reflection of our own self-judgment.

SOLUTION

When it comes to minimizing the impact of our appearance obsession on our relationships, the first step involves separating our own appearance doubts and insecurities from others' expectations and feedback. As we have seen, we are the ones who are likely to have the highest appearance expectations for ourselves. At a swimsuit party we may be sure that our date is zooming in on the cellulite on the back of our legs; yet, because men tend to view attractiveness from a "whole person" point of view, this is highly unlikely. What is likely is that our own self-consciousness about this part of our anatomy is creating this fear.

The second step is to communicate clearly with others how their statements, suggestions or feedback is affecting you. As we have seen, there is a real pressure to look good in our society. If our friends or colleagues are insecure about their own looks, they may choose to distract themselves by focusing on our looks. If this happens often, we may need to let the other person know that this feedback is not welcome.

The third step is recognizing that self-improvement concerning looks is a personal choice, not a relationship mandate. No matter how another person wants us to look, the decision is ours. We should not let others make these choices for us, nor should we attempt to control these choices in others.

Who Influences You?

The extent to which "looks messages" from others directly influence our behavior and our self-esteem is likely to be related to the power we give the message-sender. We may become particularly sensitive to feedback from others, especially if a person is very important to us. If we are not comfortable with our own appearance, praise from others can quickly turn into internal pressure to continue our self-improvement routine, and criticism may leave us feeling depressed and inadequate.

Exercise: How Others Influence Your Appearance

Rank in order from one to six how much influence each of the following groups has on you in terms of your appearance. For example, a one would be the group whose feedback is the most important to you, and a six would be the least important.

_____ my parents or siblings

_____ work colleagues

_____ friends of the same sex

_____ friends of the opposite sex

_____ date, spouse or significant other

_____ others (for example: these may include other people at the gym or members of a support group)

Now that you have determined which individuals have the most influence on you, evaluate how often and what kind of messages you usually get from them. If you would say that your most important group makes very frequent comments about your looks, or if the messages you get are often negative, it is time to take some action. In Chapter 9, we will look at ways to prevent feedback from influencing your body image or your behavior. Regardless of how these messages affect your behavior, read on for some specific communication strategies that will help you interact differently with others about your appearance.

Couple Battles: Communicating About Looks

Here are some of the couples' struggles that I have observed concerning appearance and some solutions that have worked:

PULLING FOR REASSURANCE

Cindy and Mike came into therapy to work out a number of relationship concerns. While we were reviewing some individual and relationship goals, Cindy began talking about her dissatisfaction with her appearance, specifically her weight. As she talked about her unhappiness and (of course) beat herself up for her "lack of willpower," she occasionally glanced at Mike, who began to look away and fidget.

Cindy's genuine pain over her negative body image was evident. It also seemed obvious to me that she was seeking some reassurance from her husband about her appearance. At the end of Cindy's report, Mike calmly leaned over and suggested that she give Weight Watcher's a try. As you can probably imagine, Cindy heard this feedback as confirmation that she did indeed have a "weight problem," and the sparks began to fly.

SOLUTION

Although this book is not about different communication styles between men and women, I firmly believe that two gender communication differences between men and women often exacerbate appearance concerns in relationships. Understanding these can help us avoid personalizing comments or miscommunications, and can lay the foundation for clearer understanding about looks.

First, men are socialized to approach what they perceive as problems by providing a solution or giving advice, while women often respond by giving emotional support. Mike's response to Cindy's struggle with her body dissatisfaction was an effort to provide assistance. His way of being involved was to help her find a solution to her pain. Just as naturally, Cindy misinterpreted this. She wanted Mike's reassurance that she looked "good" to him and some sympathy for the struggle she was going through.

As the session progressed, Mike stated that he was satisfied with Cindy's appearance and that he just wanted her to feel better about herself. He also noted that he felt helpless when Cindy talked about her unhappiness, and didn't know what to do. Cindy seemed surprised to hear this and told Mike that she sometimes just wanted him to listen to her. As the communication improved, Cindy began to focus on her individual appearance obsession and work on getting a better body image for herself.

Second, men are less likely than women to seek praise and to give praise. This has nothing to do with what our significant other thinks of the way we look; it is a communication style difference that has been documented over and over again. While it can be frustrating when our significant other doesn't comment on our brand-new outfit, it doesn't necessarily mean that he hasn't noticed it. There is nothing wrong with wanting compliments or positive feedback from a significant other. Our chances might be better, however, if we asked for them directly.

OUR FAMILIES REVISITED

Jack and Kelly got into appearance battle after appearance battle. As a child Jack had been overweight and had received a considerable amount of negative attention from his thin, looks-conscious mother. His father had struggled repeatedly with his own weight, and he recalled his mother attempting to "help" his father with his diet and exercise.

Jack met Kelly at a health club and was instantly attracted to what he termed her "discipline" and "willpower." At the time he met her, he was on a self-described "roll" in terms of his diet and exercise. Kelly had a long history of weight training and aerobics activity, and seemed very confident with her looks. She often wore sexy clothes and she got along well and easily with his male friends. As their relationship progressed, however, some of these initial sources of attraction became appearance battlegrounds.

During a period of stress, Jack put on some weight and had much less time to exercise. Because his physical appearance was heavily tied to his self-esteem, he began to feel more and more insecure about himself. These feelings began to surface in a number of ways in his relationship.

Jack began to feel threatened by Kelly's looks, and he began to criticize her appearance. He attempted to change her clothes to a more conservative style because he found her "sexy" appearance suddenly threatening. He also became jealous. Kelly responded in kind, "teasing" him about his weight gain and often commenting on the "powerful" physiques of the men she saw at the gym. Underneath, though, old appearance insecurities surfaced as Jack's critical remarks reminded her of her unattractive teenage years. She attempted to hide this pain through more exercise and weight control. In this way, individual appearance concerns became relationship concerns.

SOLUTION

Jack and Kelly genuinely cared about each other. Their first step in resolving their appearance conflicts was to agree to stop making negative comments to each other and to quit trying to control personal choices, such as diet or clothes style. After making this pact, they began to explore underlying fears that were being channeled into appearance concerns. Because our society is so appearance focused, we sometimes have to address the surface problem before we can look deeper.

SOMETIMES NOTHING WORKS

What about involvement in a relationship where appearance continues to be a battle? The way we look, and how we feel about it, is our own concern. The more we work on building up our own appearance security and develop a healthy and comfortable balance between self-improvement and self-acceptance, the less vulnerable we are to feedback from others.

This doesn't mean, however, that we should accept, or continue to be involved with, people who continually criticize us or attempt to make us feel bad about the way we look. Recognizing the underlying insecurity in someone else that triggers criticism doesn't mean accepting hurtful behavior. When this becomes a pattern that continues despite repeated feedback about the pain and hurt that it causes, it may be time to walk away.

Some signs that you may seriously need to evaluate your relationship are when your significant other:

• pushes you to get plastic surgery that you don't want

- tries to control or monitor your eating or exercise
- repeatedly makes critical comments about your looks or body size
- frequently makes negative comparisons between you and other members of your gender
- attempts to change or dictate your choice in clothes

When we grow up in an environment where looks are either excessively emphasized or negatively critiqued, we may be attracted to partners in adulthood who continue this pattern. As we play out these issues in relationships, our underlying appearance obsession can get lost. Sometimes we need to address the relationship problems before we can begin serious work on our appearance obsession.

A Final Thought About Relationships

As we have seen throughout this chapter, our appearance obsession not only affects how we view ourselves, it affects our relationships with others — directly and indirectly. Bombarded with societal messages about the importance of looks, we may see and feel appearance pressures everywhere. As a result, it can be difficult to separate our inside pressures and concerns from our interactions and relationships with others. With some attention, however, it can be done!

Once you have separated your personal struggles from your relationships you are left with yourself. You may have already begun to realize that feelings of insecurity or jealousy are not a symptom of relationship trouble but instead point to your low opinion of yourself. You may be wondering what part your looks play in this lowered opinion; surely beautiful people don't painfully compare themselves to others or feel anxious in social situations! Turn to the next chapter to see the relationship between looking good and feeling good — and what you can do about both.

IF I LOOK
GOOD, WILL I
FEEL GOOD?

When a woman gets up to speak, people look; then if they like what they see, they listen.

Pauline Frederick

Do people pay more attention to attractive women? With our society's emphasis on physical appearance, we naturally associate beauty with power. We look at a top model such as Cindy Crawford and fantasize about the glamorous life she must lead. The hope that our lives will improve if we look better may fuel our continued self-improvement efforts. We may motivate ourselves with dreams of romantic popularity, improved self-confidence and more exciting lives.

Many of my clients are convinced that their lives would dramatically improve if they were more attractive. They put off plans until they lose weight and cling to their self-improvement efforts as insurance that someday their lives will get better. They talk with envy about attractive men and women, and easily attribute the good fortunes of others to their physical attractiveness. They are sure that good-looking women never have self-doubts, anxiety or a lapse in self-confidence.

For instance, one of my clients, Pat, secretly responded with anger when a colleague admitted to feelings of uncertainty about an upcoming job review. "What has she got to worry about? With her looks the promotion is in the bag. She'll never have to work as hard as I do to get what she wants in life." My client dismissed her colleague's actual job performance as a consideration in the outcome of her evaluation. Sadly, she also tends to belittle her own valuable assets.

At times, Pat links her less-than-satisfactory social life, her low self-esteem and her dissatisfaction with her job to her looks. She attributes romantic disappointments to her body size. She overlooks other factors, such as her fears of making changes in her life and her lack of trust in her ability to make good decisions.

What, if any, are the real benefits of physical attractiveness? How much focus on self-improvement is enough, and where does self-acceptance begin? What about plastic surgery — will it change your life for the better, or is it another appearance trap? The answers to these questions will provide a foundation by which you can realistically examine and choose the role that looks have in your life, and the amount of time and energy you commit to improving your personal appearance.

Beauty Stereotypes

When we meet someone new, neither of us starts with a clean slate. We each bring certain assumptions about the other to our initial meeting. These assumptions may be based on our personal histories; for instance, if we have just gotten out of a very painful romantic relationship, we may find ourselves eyeing new dating partners with distrust. Personal histories aside, our assumptions may also arise from attitudes and beliefs we have been taught from an early age.

Our commonly held assumptions, or *stereotypes*, may include beliefs that certain groups of people who share one characteristic (such as race, gender or age) also share other characteristics. Whether or not they are actually true, they lead us to approach each new person with a certain mindset that influences how we treat this person and how we interpret his or her interactions with us.

If we assume that a good-looking person is also sociable or naturally intelligent, our attitude will influence the way we behave. We may try harder to be outgoing, or we may start out by engaging in a stimulating intellectual discussion.

Not only do our assumptions influence the way we behave, they also influence how we interpret the behavior of the other person. We are more likely to pay attention to things they do that confirm these initial assumptions, and are likely to pay less attention to things that do not conform to our expectations. Thus, our initial mindset can create a circular effect — if we assume good things about a person, we are likely to get these good things, and this further confirms our initially positive attitude.

BEAUTY MAKES A GOOD IMPRESSION

When we first meet a good-looking person, we tend to assume that good looks on the outside equals good qualities on the inside. This is the "beauty is good" stereotype. We tend to think good-looking people "have it all" — good social skills, assertiveness, high self-esteem and emotional stability.

These assumptions clearly contribute to making a good first impression. In fact, it is during first impressions, and in most social situations, that good-looking people tend to profit most. When we have little or no information about a person, physical attractiveness is likely to provide an advantage. Some studies indicate that attractive people find it easier to get a job, can persuade others to help them more easily and are exposed to more dating and social opportunities. At the outset, then, good-looking people often do have an edge in the interpersonal arena.

THE OTHER SIDE OF GOOD LOOKS

So far, it may seem that continual self-improvement might well be worth the effort. Maybe our lives *would* be better if we were exceptionally good-looking.

There is another side to this story. Being good-looking in our society also carries some pretty heavy responsibilities and, for many individuals, some enormous pressures. For instance, while attractive individuals may have an initial advantage in terms of the job selection process, attractive people, both men and women, are often judged more harshly in terms of their job performance. Attractive women in nontraditional jobs have the most difficult time; because we often associate beauty with femininity, attractive women have a harder time establishing credibility in a traditionally masculine profession such as law or medicine, regardless of their actual performance.

Good-looking people also may have trouble trusting other people to see beyond their looks to other qualities. As our looks are less under our control than many other characteristics, this can lead to insecurity and self-doubts. In one study, attractive men and women who were observed by others on an achievement task felt less secure of their success and tended to believe that others judged them more by their looks than by their actual performance.

Physical attractiveness for both men and women is often associated with public self-consciousness, that is, they tend to be highly aware of themselves in terms of how they appear to others, and less aware of their inner thoughts and feelings. Given the attention good looks commands in our society, this is not surprising.

In addition, we tend to have some less-than-positive associations toward physically attractive individuals. Modesty, for example, is a characteristic that is *not* associated with physical attractiveness, yet it is one that is generally valued in our culture. At a certain point, attractiveness can even be a minus. Moderately attractive people tend to have the most social advantages, while exceptionally good-looking people are often seen as vain and shallow.

Why do these stereotypes exist? One obvious link is the entertainment media. As we saw in Chapter 3, there is an unrealistic proportion of culturally attractive people on TV shows and in magazines, and we invest them with an unrealistic halo of glamour. Think for a minute about soap opera characters — not only are the men and women exceptionally attractive, they exude sexuality and charm. They lead exciting, even dangerous lives, and have numerous sexual interests and affairs. These associations perpetuate the stereotype of the "beautiful" people who are confident, sexual and sophisticated. Behind the glossy masks, however, we see a different reality.

BEYOND THE STEREOTYPE

As we have seen, stereotypes associated with good looks in our society carry some pluses and some minuses. We can argue the relative weight of these pluses and minuses or, like most of the people I know, we may already think the pluses far outweigh the minuses. What may be more important to consider, however, is whether there is a real basis for *any* assumptions or stereotypes based on the way a person looks.

Research indicates that there doesn't appear to be much. In fact, the only consistent findings are that, as a group, physically attractive people tend to be less anxious in social situations and to report less loneliness. By preschool, both teachers and peers rate physically attractive children as more popular and more effective. Because of this, some researchers propose that physically attractive individuals are exposed to more social situations and therefore have more opportunities to develop effective social skills.

Being at ease with others provides its own benefits. Not only do we believe that physically attractive people have good social skills, we also tend to rate socially competent individuals as more attractive.

Other than having more social opportunities and being more comfortable in social situations, however, research repeatedly reveals that there are *no* inherent advantages to good looks. In addition, there is *no* relationship between a person's outward appearance and his or her personality. Physically attractive people are no more assertive, outgoing or mentally healthy than less attractive individuals. As a group they also do not have a higher level of self-esteem.

My work counseling very attractive models as they struggle with their low self-worth corroborates this research. No matter how attractive others think we are, outward physical attractiveness has very little to do with how we feel about ourselves or how we judge our own attractiveness.

Why Don't Beautiful People Have It All?

Looking good does not automatically translate into feeling good. In fact, there is very little relationship between the two. In spite of our assumptions about good-looking people and the initial social advantages they may have, they are as individual as the rest of us. They struggle with the same insecurities, self-esteem issues and relationship challenges that everyone else does. If Pat's fantasies of a different look were realized, she might be disappointed with the results.

Intuitively this may not make much sense. We have seen that children who are "cute" or "pretty" command more attention and are exposed to more social situations than children who are considered less attractive. Surely adult men and women who fit our culture's beauty standards will be rewarded and will be more likely to develop a healthy sense of self-worth. So why don't they?

The answer is that there is little relationship between objective physical attractiveness (attractiveness as viewed by others) and self-perceived attractiveness. Men and women who receive high marks for good looks don't necessarily see themselves as attractive. Don't you have a very attractive friend who never seems satisfied with his or her looks? Perhaps you know someone who is of normal weight who complains of "feeling fat." If we are struggling with our own appearance concerns, a natural reaction is to feel angry or to discount that person's feelings. What does *she* (or *he*) have to complain about?

Yet this person's thoughts and feelings represent his or her reality. Many factors determine our perception of our attractiveness. While outward physical attractiveness carries some social benefits, self-perceived physical attractiveness carries emotional pluses across the board.

WHAT *YOU* SEE MAKES THE DIFFERENCE

How good-looking do you think you are? How attractive do you feel? Your answers to these questions will help you determine your personal sense of attractiveness.

Right now, let's see how you rate yourself — not your internal body image, but your *objective* rating. These two can be quite different; I have seen many models who rate themselves objectively as an "8" or a "9," yet carry around a chronic dissatisfaction with the way they look. With the perfect "10s" staring at us from every magazine stand, a high self-rating is no guarantee of a positive body image. For now, just decide what rating you would give yourself on the following scale, regardless of your feelings about it:

Figure 9.1. Objective Body Rating Scale

1	2	3	4	5	6	7	8	9	10
I				I					I
very unattractive				average attractiveness					very attractive

What would it take to move you toward the higher end of the personal attractiveness scale? Many of us think that it would require a change in our looks. Yet the evidence reveals that objective attractiveness has little to do with subjective good looks. What does directly influence our personal sense of attractiveness may surprise you.

The key appears to be a healthy self-esteem. In fact, a stable sense of self-esteem is the single factor most likely to result in a personal sense of attractiveness. Regardless of your personal decisions about self-improvement, working on your own level of self-esteem will have the greatest effect on your own attractiveness rating. When it comes to feeling good about the way we look, investing time and energy into building our self-esteem is much more beneficial than trying to improve our looks.

Self-confidence and self-respect are directly related to our overall sense of emotional well-being. Not only does it improve our appearance satisfaction, this overall sense of well-being carries over into our relationships with others. When *we* feel good about the way we look, we are likely to be more outgoing, assertive and comfortable in our interactions with others. These qualities are all things that others find attractive. And while we do not have direct control over our looks, there are some specific steps we can take to lift our self-esteem.

SELF-ESTEEM: MANY PARTS MAKE A WHOLE

Self-esteem is probably the most popular concept in psychology today. But what is it really? Many experts divide self-esteem into two factors: self-confidence and self-respect. Self-confidence is our belief in our ability to do things, to take action to change our circumstances and to meet our goals. Self-respect is the degree to which we think we deserve to be happy, to have rewarding relationships, to stand up for our rights, goals and values.

As many of us can testify, self-respect and self-confidence are not absolutes. And neither is self-esteem. We may have confidence in some areas, but less in others. We may respect (and stand up for) ourselves at work, but consistently find ourselves valuing the needs and desires of our romantic partner over our own.

This is because our self-esteem is made up of many different parts of ourselves. In Chapter 8, for instance, we talked about social esteem, the degree to which we feel confident and comfortable in social situations. Much of this book has focused on our body esteem — the value and importance we give our looks. We all have a certain amount of esteem invested in a number of areas of our lives — in our friendships, in our work, in our looks, in our romantic relationships and so forth.

Figure 9.2. Self-Esteem: Many Parts Make A Whole

Figure 9.2. illustrates several common components of our over-all self-esteem. However, the slices are different for each of us. For instance, if we place a high value on our intelligence, the "smart" slice may take up a lot of room. We will put a lot of energy into achievement and activities that confirm the fact that we are smart. For us, intelligence is a strong value point. Information that either confirms or shakes this valued quality is likely to have a big impact on us (see Figure 9.3 below.).

Figure 9.3. Self-Esteem: All Parts Are Not Equal

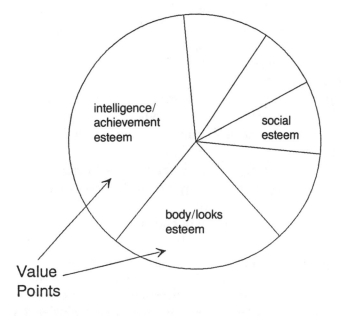

As we saw in Chapter 4, we can predict the self-esteem of a teenage girl by assessing her body esteem. Because society places so much emphasis on physical appearance our looks are likely to be a major value point for most of us. It's no wonder that we are highly sensitive to comments about our looks or that we frequently compare ourselves to others.

WHEN OUR SELF-ESTEEM IS VULNERABLE

Sometimes our value points turn into vulnerabilities. Just because we place a high value on a certain aspect of ourselves doesn't necessarily mean that we feel good about that part. For instance, if our physical appearance is very important to us, yet we don't feel secure in the way we look, this value point may cause tremendous conflict and pain. We may be highly successful in our careers and others may perceive us as having it all together. Underneath, however, we may suffer from a shaky self-esteem.

A shaky self-esteem is one that is highly influenced by outside circumstances. It changes easily and often in response to external events and feedback. One day we feel confident, the next day we feel insecure. Do you ever feel puzzled by rapid changes in your sense of self-worth? One of my clients summed up her fluctuating self-esteem by saying, "How can I feel so good about myself one day and so bad the next?"

The root of a vulnerable self-esteem is our reliance on outside approval to feel good about ourselves. When we are getting confirmation from the outside, everything is okay, our self-esteem is intact; if we were to take a self-esteem quiz, we would score fairly high. In fact, if we are overly dependent on outside approval, good things that happen to us may create feelings of euphoria and joy.

The high that we may get from outside confirmation is equaled by our incredible lows when this confirmation is unavailable. When outside confirmation disappears, or changes, so does our own sense of self-worth. Even the routine stress of daily life affects our own view and value of ourselves; a critical remark from the boss may send us into hours of depression. We may work even harder to get those outside sources of approval, providing us with temporary relief. Yet the underlying pattern remains, and will reoccur the next time our sources of approval are removed.

Everyone has normal fluctuations in self-esteem. None of us enjoys criticism, and we certainly do (and should) enjoy the positive things that come our way. We all have feelings about things that happen to us. It is only when we have dramatic mood (and self-esteem) changes in response to outside events that we have cause for concern. Even if the dramatic mood change is in a positive direction, we can be sure that the higher our high is, the lower our lows can go (see Figure 9.4.).

ADDITIONAL SELF-ESTEEM RISK FACTORS

Two additional factors leave us at risk for a shaky self-esteem. First, when our self-worth is based on a few value points, we have fewer sources of confirmation. When our pie has only two slices in it, taking one away leaves a big gap. I can certainly relate to that one.

As I shared with you in Chapter 1, my two sources of self-esteem while growing up were looks and intelligence. Both often depended on outside sources — I relied heavily on positive feedback from others in the "looks department," and tended to judge my intelligence based on my grades. These two were certainly better than having a single source of self-esteem, and I was fortunate that one source of self-esteem was continually present. However, I can only imagine the self-esteem struggle I would have encountered had I experienced difficulty in both areas at the same time.

The second risk factor is basing our self-esteem on our relationships. Our friendships and romantic relationships can be valuable sources of emotional support for us. When we're going through tough times, our relationships with others can help us get through them. However, while we obviously have influence in our relationships with others, we never have total control. When we let our self-esteem be determined by what happens in our relationships with others, we are running the risk of having the rug pulled out from under us.

For a while a friend of mine judged her self-esteem and her personal sense of attractiveness (remember how closely these two are linked) on whether or not she was in a romantic relationship. As her middle thirties approached, she began to worry about getting older and she found herself relying on the responsiveness of men in her social circle to provide her with information about how she was doing in the aging process.

Figure 9.4. Vulnerable vs. Stable Self-Esteem

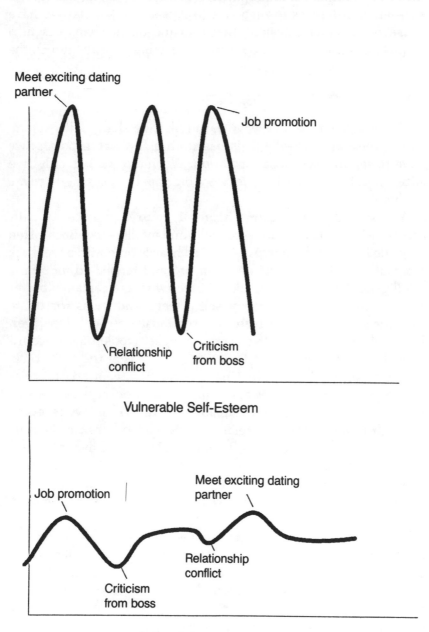

A new date signaled confirmation of her attractiveness, a romantic disappointment sent her into a self-esteem tailspin. As she
began to look at her underlying concerns, such as her desire to
get married and start a family and her fears that this might not
happen, she went through a painful period of introspection. She
began to realize that, like most of us, she had always gone through
periods of dating and, as she called them, "dry spells." The only
difference was that her inside fears and concerns were causing
her to interpret outside events differently. And because of her
different interpretation of the same events, she was feeling bad
about herself. She emerged with a clearer sense of what she
wanted and regained control over feeling good about herself.

Is Your Self-Esteem On A Roller Coaster?

On a separate sheet of paper — because you will be taking this test
again — answer the following questions. Circle the letter that best
describes how you feel today.

1. It is easy for me to accept compliments.
   A = never B = rarely C = sometimes D = often E = almost always

2. I believe it is important for me to be truly outstanding at something.
   A = never B = rarely C = sometimes D = often E = almost always

3. I find myself dwelling on past mistakes I have made.
   A = never B = rarely C = sometimes D = often E = almost always

4. If I can't do something very well, I would rather not do it.
   A = never B = rarely C = sometimes D = often E = almost always

5. If I have to ask for help, it is a sign of weakness.
   A = never B = rarely C = sometimes D = often E = almost always

6. When I make a mistake, I view it as an opportunity to learn rather
   than a personal failure.
   A = never B = rarely C = sometimes D = often E = almost always

7. I have a hard time letting go of criticism.
   A = never B = rarely C = sometimes D = often E = almost always

8. If someone disagrees with me, I tend to think they don't like me.
   A = never B = rarely C = sometimes D = often E = almost always

9. I trust myself to make the right decisions.
   A = never   B = rarely   C = sometimes   D = often   E = almost always

10. It is hard for me to acknowledge some of my feelings, even to myself.
    A = never   B = rarely   C = sometimes   D = often   E = almost always

11. I am critical of myself (beat myself up, often feel guilty).
    A = never   B = rarely   C = sometimes   D = often   E = almost always

12. I am very sensitive to the comments that others make.
    A = never   B = rarely   C = sometimes   D = often   E = almost always

Scoring: For questions 1, 6 and 9, give yourself one point if you answered A, two points if you answered B, three points if you answered C, four points if you answered D and five points if you answered E.

For questions 2, 3, 4, 5, 7, 8, 10, 11 and 12, give yourself five points if you answered A, four points if you answered B, three points if you answered C, two points if you answered D and one point if you answered E.

Add up your total score:

48–60: High Self-Esteem. Your score indicates that you are currently placing a high value on yourself. You are likely to put outside feedback in perspective and to have realistic expectations of yourself. Take a minute to appreciate your good feelings about yourself. Follow the tracking exercise at the end of this section to see how firm this good foundation is.

30–47: Moderate Self-Esteem. Your score suggests that your current self-esteem is in the moderate range. Look at your pattern of answers to see what areas need strengthening, and what areas are strong points for you. Use the following pattern analysis; the tracking exercise that follows will also help you.

- If you answered "often" or "almost always" to 7, 8 and 12: evaluate your relationship value point — you may be giving too much influence to others.
- If you answered "often" or "almost always" to 4, 5, 6 and 9: evaluate your achievement value point — you may be creating unrealistic expectations for yourself.
- If you answered "often" or "almost always" to 1, 3, 10 and 11: evaluate your internal dialogue — the way you interpret events may be causing you difficulty.

12–29: Low Self-Esteem. What's wrong? Your score indicates that you are currently feeling pretty bad about yourself. Is your low self-evaluation a response to something that has happened recently, or is it characteristic of how you normally feel? Do the tracking exercise that follows to help you sort this out. In addition, you might refer to some of the resources at the end of this book if these painful feelings continue.

Tracking Exercise:

Come back to this questionnaire and redo it four times over the next three weeks. If your score fluctuates by ten points or more, you may be suffering from shaky self-esteem.

STRENGTHENING YOUR SELF-ESTEEM

If your self-esteem is currently shaky, you can begin now to strengthen it. Here are some strategies that work.

Identify And Expand Your Value Points

It is not what happens to us, but how we interpret and respond to it that matters. It is hard to believe this when we are in the midst of a personal crisis, but it's true. Even individuals who experience a major catastrophe, such as a life-threatening illness or the death of a loved one, show amazingly varied psychological and behavioral responses.

You have more control over the impact of painful events on your self-esteem than you may think. The more aware you are of your vulnerable areas — value points that are very important to you — the easier it will be to identify situations that are likely to be triggers.

Monitor your self-esteem over the next three weeks. If you notice a significant drop, write down what was happening that day. What triggered your low evaluation of yourself? Ask yourself the following questions:

- What am I letting this say about me?
- How would I interpret this event if it happened to a close friend?
- What do I want to do about it?
- How can I handle it if it happens again?

Another way to reduce the impact of your triggers is to expand your value points. Work to make the slices in your pie more even. Value yourself for your honesty, your creativity, your dependability. Appreciate the factors you have control over (your effort, your courage to try new things, your preparation) regardless of the outcome. If you work to value your many real assets, and enjoy your progress in other areas of your life, a letdown in one area will have less impact.

Identify And Change Internal Messages

While we all have feelings about things that happen to us, we don't have to let them affect our self-worth. A clue that outside influences are becoming too important is when we respond to these events with statements about ourselves: a date suddenly drops out of the picture and we interpret this as an indication that we are not interesting or attractive. We make a mistake at work and tell ourselves that we are a failure.

Numerous self-help books are devoted to improving our self-talk. There's a good reason; researchers who have attempted to sort out the numerous factors related to stress found that self-deprecation — putting oneself down — was the number-one predictor of stress for men and women. Freedom from negative self-talk, on the other hand, will allow you to view events and your feelings about them as objective information. You can then decide what you want to do about them.

Evaluate Your Expectations

Expanding our value points is not the same as expanding our roles or our activities. It means valuing our many assets, and appreciating the many things we do every day. In fact, too many roles or activities can lower our self-esteem if we expect perfection in each of them.

We've already seen how comparing our looks to the beauty ideals fostered by the media inevitably results in frustration and dissatisfaction. When we extend these unrealistically high expectations to other areas of our lives, the results are likely to be the same. We may expend enormous amounts of energy, yet never be satisfied with the outcome. Or we may be so afraid of making a mistake or failing that we don't venture out at all. Regardless of the impact on our behavior, the emotional toll is high.

Evaluating and adjusting your expectations means appreciating your progress rather than striving for perfection. It means rewarding yourself for your efforts rather than the outcome. It also means evaluating your goals and priorities realistically and deciding what is good enough.

Acting "As If," Even If You Don't

Suppose you've had a really tough day. You're tired and frustrated, and those self-critical tapes have kicked in. You find yourself replaying something that happened on this day over and over again, and beating yourself up for the way you handled it. Suddenly your best friend calls, crying, and says she is in trouble and needs your help. What would you do?

Most of us, no matter how we feel, would respond. Even if we didn't feel like it, we would try to help as best we could. Why is it so hard to do these same things for ourselves? Sometimes it seems like when we need to nurture ourselves the most we do it the least.

Most often, we think of self-esteem as a feeling. Yet it also comes from how we treat ourselves, the things we do. Even if sometimes we don't feel like it, one of the best ways we can begin to stabilize our self-esteem is to do, consistently, two self-nurturing activities a week — activities that don't require work and that are not related to self-improvement. What is considered self-nurturing varies for each of us. Some of the items my clients have shared from their self-nurturing list include:

- a massage
- a bubble bath
- watching the sun set
- reading spiritual or inspirational material
- writing poetry or painting
- dining by candlelight

What two self-nurturing activities will you do next week?

Age, Looks And Self-Esteem

Youth and beauty. For Americans, these two are often closely tied together. Normal physical signs of aging are all too often judged as an indication of diminished attractiveness and lower abilities. As a result, these physical changes may be viewed as a challenge to overcome. When 16-year-old girls are modeling "wrinkle-free" cosmetics, we may react to our laugh lines with insecurity and fear.

As we saw in Chapter 7, women are often viewed as less attractive as they get older. Men also worry about getting older, and are likely to be sensitive to information that suggests diminished abilities. Getting winded on the softball field may create anxiety in a middle-aged male who interprets this as an inevitable consequence of age.

With our cultural emphasis on youth, and our body esteem so closely tied to our self-esteem, we might naturally assume that increasing age will inevitably lead to a drop in our self-value. This is not necessarily so. In fact, many studies show that self-esteem actually rises with age. Having a base of experience can help us put many things in perspective, including our appearance.

In my research, older survey respondents tended to feel more secure about their looks. While they were more likely to color their hair, older men and women were less likely to compare their looks to others'. They also tended to be less sensitive to comments about their looks, and endorsed items indicating an easier ability to present their "true" selves to others.

These findings suggest that getting older may actually tend to promote a greater degree of appearance security. Our interest in being attractive doesn't necessarily diminish (and women continue to be more concerned about their looks than men throughout their lifespan). However, the influence of this interest on our self-esteem does diminish.

There is a catch though. The more we rely on our looks when we are younger, the harder it may be to accept the physical changes that come with age. Attractive women tend to have a harder time with the physical changes associated with age; research indicates that women who were very attractive at age 20 (and undoubtedly are very attractive at 40), report more dissatisfaction with their appearance as they get older. In a study of men's reactions to baldness, researchers found that the more a man was concerned about his looks prior to his baldness, the more upset he was after he started losing his hair. The actual extent of his hair loss had little to do with his reaction to it. Putting our looks in perspective when we are younger appears to have long-term benefits.

The Plastic Surgery Debate

Plastic surgery is a personal choice and, as we have already seen, an increasingly popular option for both men and women. In my study, 16 percent of the women surveyed and 2 percent of the men had undergone plastic surgery. Among plastic surgery recipients, 75 percent are women and 25 percent are men.

The stance health professionals have taken toward plastic surgery candidates has changed with the times. Even ten years ago, men who sought plastic surgery were viewed with suspicion and thought to have underlying "emotional problems." As more and more men have sought plastic surgery, this choice has become more "normal." Today, an increasing number of men are getting plastic surgery for business reasons, in an attempt to look younger and stronger in a highly competitive job market. These factors are motivators for women in the workplace, too.

Before you make a decision about plastic surgery, build a firm foundation of self-worth. Not only does stable self-esteem enhance our personal sense of attractiveness, it can also help us to develop realistic expectations about what plastic surgery will *and* won't do for us.

The benefits associated with plastic surgery depend on how you feel about yourself beforehand, and how you feel about the outcome. Most people say they are pleased with the results of their plastic surgery. Yet people who seek plastic surgery are not less physically attractive than people who don't. In one study, for instance, raters were unable to distinguish a group of plastic surgery candidates from a control group. What did distinguish plastic surgery candidates from others was a higher level of appearance dissatisfaction.

What do these confusing findings suggest? That our own perception of our looks is what matters. If we are unhappy with one body part, regardless of how it looks to others, plastic surgery might raise our own estimation of our looks even when others thought we were attractive all along.

On the other hand, plastic surgery does not cure a chronic dissatisfaction with our appearance. Janet's story firmly attests to this fact. As a 22-year-old, she had long been disgusted with what she called her "thunder thighs and hippo hips." At age 23,

she had liposuction to "correct" this part of her anatomy. She was
very pleased with the results — for a while. After several months,
however, she began talking about the "fat" on other body parts
which were satisfactory to her before. She began considering
liposuction for other body areas.

One of the risks associated with plastic surgery, I believe, is
that it can become an increasingly easy option and even somewhat
addictive. I know several women who dreamed of being able to
wear a size-C bra. Yet once they had adjusted to their breast
implants, they wanted larger ones — and subsequently sought
additional plastic surgery to accommodate their higher goals.

Before you seek plastic surgery, ask yourself the following questions:

1. *Is this something you want?*
   Consider: A decision to seek plastic surgery should be yours, and
   yours alone. This decision should never be made out of a desire to
   please someone else, and pressure from a significant other signals
   a need to examine the relationship closely. Remember, relationships can come and go, but you are the one who has to live with
   the results.

2. *Are your expectations realistic?*
   Consider: Do you dream about a new life, more dates or career
   advantages as plausible outcomes from plastic surgery? If so, it
   might be time to address some of the areas of your life that you
   are dissatisfied with first, then re-evaluate plastic surgery as an
   option.

3. *How long have you been considering plastic surgery?*
   Consider: Because plastic surgery is a relatively permanent procedure, I believe that the decision process should be a slow one. Few
   people regret postponing a major decision temporarily, while impulsive acts can lead to regrets.

4. *What else is going on in your life?*
   Consider: If you are depressed, or are undergoing a personal crisis,
   now is *not* the time to opt for plastic surgery. It is difficult to make
   rational choices when we are in emotional pain. Delay your decision for six months. Once you are feeling better or your crisis has
   been resolved, think about it again.

5. *Do you have all the information you need?*
   Consider: As with any surgical procedure there are risks involved.
   Make sure you know what they are, and have talked with other

people who have had the same procedure, before you make your final decision. A good decision is an informed one.

6. *Have you had plastic surgery before?*
   Consider: Multiple plastic surgeries may signal that something other than your appearance is wrong. It may be helpful to talk to a mental health professional if you find yourself repeatedly considering plastic surgery. This is especially true if, like Janet, "successful" plastic surgery on one body part leads to an increased dissatisfaction with others.

7. *Is your decision fashion-motivated?*
   Consider: The "face of the seventies" was not the "face of the eighties." And the face of the nineties is likely to change as the decade progresses. Make sure that you will be happy with your decision over the long haul. With our rapidly changing beauty standards, it might be easier (and cheaper) to wait until your face comes into style rather than trying to change it to keep up with the latest fashion.

IF YOU DECIDE TO SAY YES TO PLASTIC SURGERY

Glossy advertisements touting virtual body transformations have become the norm in some parts of the country. Many cosmetic surgery advertisements list numerous surgical procedures, yet many of the best professionals specialize in one body area. If you have decided that plastic surgery is for you, use the following guidelines to find a *qualified* plastic surgeon.

1. Ask about the surgeon's credentials and *check them out.*
2. Always get a second, and even a third, opinion.
3. Be sure the doctor has a personal consultation with you, and see whether he or she openly discusses the possible risks and complications.
4. Ask to see before and after photos of the surgical procedure you are requesting. It may be especially helpful to bring along someone you trust so you can get their opinion as well.
5. Call the hospital where the doctor has privileges and find out if the physician is credentialed for your procedure.
6. Find a personal reference if at all possible.
7. Don't make a decision during the initial consultation. Go home and think it over.
8. Make sure the doctor doesn't offer unrealistic promises during your consultation (seeing a couple of different professionals will

help you sort this out). If you have *any doubts* about your physician, choose another doctor.

9. Make sure the doctor is credentialed in the body part for which you are seeking modification.
10. Find out whether the outpatient clinic the doctor uses is credentialed for plastic surgery.

A Final Thought About Looks And Self-Esteem

This chapter has explored the myths and realities of good looks. Because of the "beauty is good" stereotype that is so prevalent in our society, physical attractiveness gives us an initial advantage during first impressions and in social situations. When other people have little additional information about us, good looks work in our favor. Not surprisingly, beauty does command attention.

Not all of this attention is positive. As we saw in Chapter 8, good-looking people often invoke feelings of jealousy and envy in others. Extremely good-looking people may be seen as vain or shallow. In addition, receiving too much attention for our looks can increase our self-consciousness when we are with others and can reduce our confidence in our abilities in other areas.

With so much outside encouragement to improve our looks, it is ironic that objective good looks bring us so little in terms of how we feel about ourselves. We are likely to feel bad about ourselves if we think we look bad, yet looking good does not necessarily mean feeling good. The key is how we rate our own level of attractiveness. In fact, as we have seen, there is a relatively small relationship between how attractive we are and how attractive we feel.

When it comes to feeling attractive, self-esteem is the foundation. Self-esteem is not something we either have or we don't have. It is composed of a number of different value points. The importance of each of our value points (such as attractiveness, relationships, achievement) in determining our overall self-worth varies for each of us depending on our cultural background, current priorities and personal histories. When one value point, such as our looks, becomes too important, we are likely to be very sensitive to circumstances and feedback relating to it. Of course we would if this one area also determines how we view the rest of ourselves!

Feeling good means starting from the inside out. It means working to build a strong sense of who we are, expanding our value points and evaluating our expectations. It also means evaluating self-improvement strategies from a realistic perspective; are we, for example, considering plastic surgery to enhance our looks or to compensate for them? Are we making the decision or are we being swayed by someone else? When we have a firm foundation of self-esteem, the answers to these questions come much more easily.

If you're like most Americans, body esteem is likely to be a strong value point for you. The barrage of beauty messages you receive from society and family can easily turn this into an area of vulnerability. As you work to expand your value points and create a stable sense of self-worth, let's look at some specific strategies for building body image in Chapter 10.

LEARNING
APPEARANCE
SECURITY

Saturday. Today I feel fat. Feels like everyone I see is staring at my stomach. I feel bloated, ugly and hopeless.

Sunday. Today everything is much brighter. I feel back in control of my life and ready to tackle my problems. I feel light; it seems like my stomach is getting smaller. I feel more like my old self, the way I used to feel.

Entries from Susan's journal, written on two consecutive days

The most outstanding feature of these writings is the dramatically different way Susan perceived and felt about her body on two sequential days. We all know that our bodies don't change in size from one day to the next. So why is it that one day we feel okay about our body shape, yet the next day we view the same body with dismay — or even disgust? In this chapter we'll explore the reasons why our body size and satisfaction are likely to fluctuate, and learn some specific steps we can take to feel secure about our appearance.

Body Image: A Three-Way Conversation

When we first think of our body image, we may assume it has to do with the way we feel about our bodies. Popular magazine articles talk about having a "positive" or a "negative" body image, suggesting that we either like our bodies or we don't. We also tend to think that our body image is based on our body. The reality is much more complex.

First, as we saw in Chapter 4, our body image initially comes from social interactions. As children and adolescents, feedback we received from others soon translated into how we saw ourselves. This feedback not only laid the groundwork for our adult body image, it also set the stage for how important our looks are to us. The greater the value we learn to place on our looks early on, the more important our looks are likely to be in adulthood.

Then there is the so-called ideal body. As we have seen, our personal body image is directly linked to our culture's beauty ideals. When we look in the mirror, we are not simply seeing our body; we are comparing our reflection to our internal model of how we are "supposed" to look. This "should look" model comes from our cultural beauty standards. This ideal body (in our mind) tells us how we are measuring up, how good we are looking by our culture's standards. Because the current beauty ideals are virtually impossible to reach, these comparisons frequently form the basis of painfully critical evaluations.

Imagine you are looking at your reflection in the mirror. While you may not be conscious of it, you are conducting a three-way conversation. On the one hand, you are comparing your present reflection to your personal body image history, the accumulation of all the reactions and feedback you have received from others and incorporated into a mental picture of the way you look. You are also evaluating your reflection in relationship to your ideal body image. This three-way interaction between your reflection, your ideal and your cumulative body image is what determines your current body image (see Figure 10.1.).

The outcome of our three-way conference with our reflection is different for each of us. This outcome, either positive or negative, is expressed in terms of how we feel and what we think about our bodies. It also influences what we actually see when we look in the mirror. As we shall see, some of us are able to judge our present body size more accurately than others. When we look at how complicated our body images really are, and how much they are influenced by our history and society, the difference between how we see ourselves and how others see us makes sense!

Figure 10.1. Body Image: A Three-Way Conversation

How We View Our Bodies: The Perceptual Component

Have you ever caught your reflection in a store window just before you realized it was you? Were you surprised by what you saw? In light of the "ideal" bodies we see on magazine covers and on TV, it is perhaps not surprising that most of us have trouble accurately judging our own body size — and we tend to err in the direction of overestimation. As we saw in Chapter 3, 95 percent of American women overestimate their body sizes by as much as 25 percent.

Beauty ideals aside, some additional factors put us at risk for body size distortion. If we have a history of yo-yo dieting and have seen the numbers on our scale repeatedly go up and down, we may have a hard time judging our body size. Similarly, if our bodies have recently changed shape through pregnancy or through a dramatic weight loss or gain, it is likely to take a while before our perceptions catch up. A history of childhood or teenage obesity is likely to add pounds to our adult size perception regardless of our present body shape.

Susan had a history of dramatic weight changes. Even after her weight stabilized, she often saw different body sizes when she looked in the mirror. Her journal entry also illustrates another common influence on our body size perception — the influence of our mood. From one day to the next, Susan's stomach seemed much smaller. From one day to the next, she felt "fat" and then much lighter. While we can be certain her body didn't change sizes, we know something did. What changed from day to day was her mood.

In my research, 69 percent of the women and 42 percent of the men said that their perception of their looks depended on the mood they were in. Thirty-eight percent of the women and 18 percent of the men strongly agreed with this body/mood connection. Because our view of our bodies is so closely linked to our view of ourselves, events and feelings that are not related to our appearance can get channeled into our looks. We may feel fat rather than depressed, ugly after a relationship breakup, or we may see a much larger person in the mirror after stepping off a scale that shows a one-pound gain. If we are not aware of the underlying trigger, we can easily go off on a self-improvement rampage in an attempt to fix our increased dissatisfaction with our appearance.

When Susan came to see me, she focused on her negative feelings about her appearance, particularly her body. She stated that she never felt good about the way she looked, and reported that this had been a constant in her life for as long as she could remember. She was also unaware of any event or feeling that influenced her view of her body, instead attributing her negative body image to an "ugly, overweight body."

When she was asked to elaborate on her "ugly body," Susan zeroed in on her stomach. She agonizingly told me how large it was, how much it stuck out, how it made her feel bloated. In fact, in talking about her body, Susan's stomach was the only body part she discussed.

Susan's selective perception is very familiar to most of us. When we look in the mirror, do we tend to do an overall assessment of our body? Do we, for example, notice how nice our lips are or spend time admiring our ankles? Probably not! Instead we tend to zoom right to the parts of our bodies that we like the least. Then we tend to generalize our overall evaluation of our bodies specifically on these areas, without stopping to notice the parts of our bodies that we like. Unfortunately, by emphasizing one body part we may be feeding a body size perception problem.

We learn at an early age to rely on our senses for feedback and information. When it comes to our body size, though, our senses can mislead us. Here are some clues that you may be distorting your body size:

- Friends describe your body size in a different way than you do.
- You feel heavier or thinner from day to day, although you know your body couldn't have changed that much overnight.
- When something upsetting happens, you react by suddenly feeling fat or unattractive.
- You have difficulty believing compliments about your looks.
- No matter how much weight you lose, you still see your body as too large.

CHANGING OUR PERCEPTIONS

Let's look at some strategies for putting our perceptions of ourselves more in line with reality.

Develop Appearance Accuracy

Without a reality check, it is difficult for any of us to know how accurate our perceptions of our bodies really are. Working

with a trusted friend can help each of you begin to develop a
more realistic perception of your body size.

Exercise: How Do You Really Look?

On large pieces of banner paper, each of you will use a colorful
magic marker to draw your own body. Doing the best you can, try
to estimate the correct size of your body. If it is helpful, look in a
mirror; focus on drawing each body part in proportion to the rest
of your body. The key is to get a picture that represents to you the
way you see your body.

Next, take turns laying down on another sheet of paper and
trace the outline of your bodies for each other. When you have
finished, place your original drawing underneath the tracing and
notice any discrepancies that are present. In particular, mark the
areas that are significantly different; this will give you information
about parts of your body with which you have the most trouble.
These are also likely to be the parts with which you are the most
dissatisfied.

Reinterpret Appearance Fluctuations

Even when we "know" that our body size does not change from
day to day, it can be hard to ignore our changing reflections in the
mirror. If we see a different body size or we see a less attractive
reflection, our feelings tend to match this perception, particularly
if we are not tuned in to what caused this perceptual change to
begin with.

It takes time to adjust our perceptions. In the beginning we
may even have to rely on an outside reality check, like a favorite
outfit or the feedback of a trusted friend. However, we can immediately begin to change the way we react to them. We can
reinterpret sudden or rapid size or attractiveness changes as
stress signals rather than painful information about our looks.

Reminding ourselves that we tend to channel our feelings into
our looks can accomplish two things. First, we can work to identify what is causing our stress, and can problem-solve ways to
address the source. If we interpret our painful perceptions as
reality, we are likely to respond by focusing on ways to improve
our looks. Seeing our appearance fluctuations as stress signals
lets us know that we need nurturing, not self-improvement.

Second, by recognizing that body size distortions give us more information about our inside than our outside, we can learn to minimize their impact on our appearance security. One of my clients, Alice, told me, "When I'm under stress, trying to accurately judge my body size or my looks is like trying to see in the dark wearing sunglasses. During these times, I temporarily rely on a comfortable outfit and work extra hard to accept compliments from others. While I am learning to get a more stable view of the way I look, it feels good to know that there are fallbacks that I can use when times are particularly tough."

Get A Holistic View

It can be hard to get an accurate view of our bodies when we notice only the parts that we don't like. I have seen many people who had a very painful relationship with their appearance; however, I have never worked with anyone who disliked every part of his or her body. The key is to teach yourself to notice all aspects of your appearance, not just the ones you dislike.

Exercise: The Holistic Mirror Check

The next time you look in the mirror, take the time to look at every body part. Start with the top of your head and go all the way to your toes. Notice your hair, the shape of your head, your skin, your facial features. What parts of your body do you like the most? Begin incorporating this holistic view into your everyday appearance check.

Body Satisfaction: Thoughts And Feelings

Getting an accurate estimate of your body size is a first step to becoming more secure with your appearance. However, as many of us are painfully aware, accuracy does not necessarily mean "ideal." And the discrepancy between the two can leave room for body dissatisfaction.

Eighty-five percent of all women and 72 percent of all men are unhappy with at least one aspect of their looks. In my research, men expressed the most dissatisfaction with their abdomens while women blasted their hip/thigh areas. Women also expressed considerably more unhappiness with and concern about their weight.

While most of us have some degree of dissatisfaction with our appearance, some of us are more dissatisfied than others. And while we are all exposed to unrealistic beauty ideals, there is considerable variability in the extent to which they personally affect each one of us. Before we look at the reasons for this variability, complete the following survey.

Perceived Discrepancy From The Ideal (PDI) And Importance Of Meeting The Ideal (IM)

A. To what extent do you feel that your body measures up to current ideal standards of attractiveness and good looks? Please indicate for each body part or function using the following scale:

1 = far below ideal
2 = below ideal
3 = average
4 = close to ideal
5 = meets ideal standard

B. How important is it to you that you meet these ideal standards? Please indicate for each body part or function using the following scale:

1 = extremely unimportant
2 = moderately unimportant
3 = no feeling one way or the other
4 = moderately important
5 = very important

Body Parts And Functions	A Discrepancy	B Importance
1. Body scent	_____	_____
2. Appetite	_____	_____
3. Nose	_____	_____
4. Physical stamina	_____	_____
5. Reflexes	_____	_____
6. Lips	_____	_____
7. Muscular strength	_____	_____
8. Waist	_____	_____

9. Energy level

10. Thighs

11. Ears

12. Biceps

13. Chin

14. Body build

15. Physical coordination

16. Buttocks

17. Agility

18. Width of shoulders

19. Arms

20. Chest or breasts

21. Appearance of eyes

22. Cheeks/cheekbones

23. Hips

24. Legs

25. Figure or physique

26. Sex drive

27. Feet

28. Sex organs

29. Appearance of stomach

30. Health

31. Sex activities

32. Body hair

33. Physical condition

34. Face

35. Weight

Reprinted with permission of Dr. Susan Kohlruss-Salem

Scoring: First, count how many body parts or functions received a 1 rating. Put a star by these. Next, for part B, add up your total score. Use the scoring system below:

111 or less: You are likely to place less emphasis on meeting our society's beauty ideals than most of us.

112–149: In a study of 161 women between the ages of 17 and 26, the average importance rating was 130. If your score falls in this range, you are not alone. However, this also means that meeting our society's beauty ideals is important to you. In particular, it will be important to look at the body parts (or functions) that you rated a 1 in part A, and a 4 or 5 in part B. Your scores on these items suggests that you are dissatisfied with these body parts, and that this dissatisfaction is in an area that is highly important to you.

150 or more: You are likely to place a great deal of emphasis on meeting our society's beauty ideals. Start with the body parts that are the most important to you and with which you are the most unhappy (look at your stars), and boost your body image with the exercises we'll discuss later in this chapter.

DISCREPANCY + IMPORTANCE = DOUBLE JEOPARDY

The greater our desire to meet cultural beauty ideals, and the less we believe that we are currently measuring up to them, the more unhappy we are likely to be. In a study by Dr. Susan Kohlruss Salem, the highest depression scores and lowest self-esteem scores occurred when current body satisfaction was low and the importance of meeting the ideal was high. When both of these occur, we are in a bind; we are trapped by our appearance pressures yet painfully aware that we aren't meeting our appearance standards.

However, the importance of meeting cultural beauty ideals was *by itself* a powerful predictor of low self-esteem and depression. If we look back at our survey, we can see how this works. For example, we might believe that our physical coordination or the width of our shoulders doesn't meet "ideal" standards. If these aren't important to us though, we can easily overlook them. On the other hand, if meeting an ideal weight is important and we find that our scales don't reflect the weight of a *Vogue* model, we may respond with depression.

This finding helps us understand why, no matter how others see us, we may find ourselves painfully obsessing about one body part or staring with disgust at our reflection in the mirror. It also suggests that placing a high degree of importance on meeting our society's beauty ideals puts us at risk for depression. In fact, as we have seen, we can easily channel our feelings into our looks. One step in reducing our emphasis on societal beauty standards is to assess our own appearance/depression connection and begin to separate our feelings from our looks.

BODY DISSATISFACTION AND DEPRESSION

There is an unquestionable relationship between depression and appearance security, particularly for women. As we saw in Chapter 4, we can get a pretty good measure of an adolescent girl's overall self-esteem by evaluating her satisfaction with her looks. As an adult, there is also a relationship between appearance satisfaction and depression. Depressive moods or thoughts are associated with body dissatisfaction; depression may lead us to focus on dissatisfaction with body parts, and dissatisfaction with body parts can result in feelings of depression.

Figure 10.2. shows the circular relationship between depression and looks dissatisfaction.

How Triggers Affect Us

As we saw at the beginning of this chapter, Susan's mood not only affected her perception of her body size, it also significantly altered her satisfaction with it. When we find our attitude toward our looks changing for the worse, it is often a sign that we may need to listen to the messages we are giving ourselves about our looks. While certain "triggers" are likely to set off negative appearance messages, it is the way we interpret them that determines how they will affect us.

Here's how this works. Imagine that you're visiting your physician for your annual checkup. The nurse greets you and, as part of the regular office routine, asks you to step on the scale. While writing your weight on your chart, she comments that you have gained a couple of pounds since your last visit.

Figure 10.2. The Appearance/Depression Connection

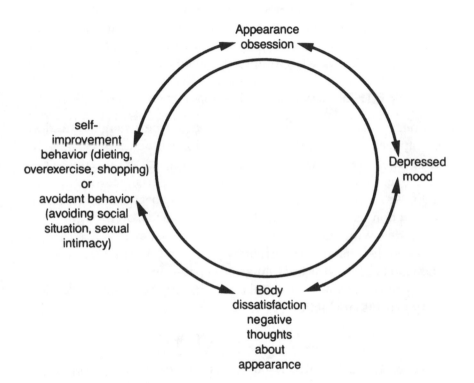

Appearance obsession

Depressed mood

Body dissatisfaction negative thoughts about appearance

self-improvement behavior (dieting, overexercise, shopping) or avoidant behavior (avoiding social situation, sexual intimacy)

Very few of us would be thrilled with these results. However, the extent of your reaction is likely to be based on your inner dialogue about this feedback. If, for example, you begin beating yourself up for your weight gain and torture yourself with fantasies of sliding, a couple of pounds at a time, into a large weight gain, your feelings are likely to match these thoughts. You might find yourself feeling depressed for the rest of the day or longer. You might vow to start a diet immediately, or find yourself overeating to console yourself for this painful experience.

Instead of reacting negatively, however, you might say some words to yourself that would lessen the impact of this feedback. For instance, you might remind yourself that your weight is within the comfortable range you have established for yourself. Or you can remind yourself that it is how your clothes fit, not what the scale says, that matters to you. Or you might recall that you felt pretty good about yourself before you came to the doctor, and reassure yourself that you were the same weight before you received this feedback. Another possibility might be to step back and observe your reaction, realizing that these painful feelings are linked to "old tapes" about the importance of weight in determining your self-image. Just by recognizing this, you can gently reaffirm your commitment to giving less "weight" to weight. All of these alternatives have two things in common: (1) they shift the power from an outside source (in this instance, the nurse's feedback and your weight gain) to an inside source (your own goals and values); and (2) they redirect painful automatic thoughts that can easily lead to a bad mood.

FOUR STEPS TO BREAKING THE APPEARANCE/DEPRESSION CONNECTION

Step 1. Identify Triggers

Throughout this book we've talked about a variety of outside events that can exacerbate our appearance obsession. In Chapter 1, for example, I related my overreaction to the attractive woman in the elevator. In Chapter 4, we discussed how appearance-related comments from our family, or present-day events that remind us of early beauty messages, can be difficult to handle. We've talked about the role of dieting, shopping and exercising, and seen how we can come to rely on these activities to make up for our painful relationship with our appearance. This overreliance makes us vulnerable: missing one day's exercise may trigger appearance dissatisfaction, or we feel unattractive if we are over-dressed or underdressed at a social event.

Some other common triggers include:

- bathing suit shopping
- weighing yourself

- relationship conflict or breakup
- work stress
- appearance-related comments from others
- loneliness or boredom
- looking in the mirror

Your personal triggers are based on your individual experiences and sensitivities. To begin identifying events that provoke painful thoughts and feelings about your appearance, keep a journal for the next two weeks. At the same time every day, write down your answers to the following questions:

1. How are you feeling about your appearance? Include any changes that occurred during the day.
2. Did you feel different about your reflection in the morning than you did in the afternoon?
3. Did you feel okay about your appearance today, but unhappy with it yesterday?

Step 2. Record Events

When you find yourself agonizing over a specific body part or focusing on a receding hairline, pay particular attention to what happened on that day. Events that can exacerbate your appearance obsession may or may not be related to appearance-related events. For some of us, a mistake at work can invoke "ugly" feelings. The important point is to find out what triggers *your* painful feelings about your appearance, and to notice when (and why) you feel better about your looks on certain days.

Step 3. Investigate Your Thoughts

Write out specific thoughts, either positive or negative, that you remember having about your appearance. What was going on right before you had those thoughts? What specific thoughts did you have? The more detailed you can be in identifying your specific thought patterns, the easier it will be to recognize them and to change them. You may be surprised to learn that you tend to tell yourself the same things over and over. The fact that you are used to these messages can at first make it hard to recognize them.

Step 4. Create New Tapes

Sometimes we have no control over the things that happen to us: a boyfriend or girlfriend leaves or we get laid off during a job restructuring. We do, however, have control over our thoughts regarding these events. When it comes to changing old appearance tapes, the key is to gently begin substituting realistic, more positive thoughts.

Creating realistic tapes means that in order for new programs to be effective, we must believe what we are telling ourselves. Jumping from "I hate my thighs" to "I look beautiful (or handsome)" will not work for most of us. However, gradually moving from "I hate my thighs" to "While I am less satisfied with my thighs than other parts of my body, I am learning to see and appreciate a lot of different parts of my appearance" might work.

The "test" in creating realistic tapes is to listen to yourself — if you have an "Oh, sure" reaction to a thought, back up and experiment with another one. As a start, try some of these:

- My looks stay the same even when I'm with people more attractive than I.
- My body may not meet the beauty ideals, but I think it's attractive.
- I'm as attractive as most people.
- The people I most admire don't look better than I do.
- My body is healthy.
- I don't have to change the way I look.

How Our Body Attitudes Influence Our Behavior

Because our body image is so closely tied to our view of ourselves, the relationship between our appearance and other important parts of our lives is often blurred. As we have seen, work or relationship matters can arouse negative feelings about our looks. In addition, having a low appearance image can spill over into how we feel about our social interactions or work accomplishments. Separating out the two can be hard, yet taking the time to do so can be invaluable.

We have already looked at several ways that we change our behavior in an attempt to cure our appearance obsession. We diet in the hope that lost weight will result in a new, improved relationship with our appearance. We exercise, we shop or we alter our bodies through plastic surgery. While these activities may temporarily reduce our appearance obsession, they don't fix the underlying problem: the pain that results from trying to live up to unreachable beauty standards. And when taken to excess, they create new problems.

Another way we can try to cope with our appearance obsession is to avoid situations that are likely to bring our appearance dissatisfaction to our attention. We may avoid social events or sexual intimacy, places where our bodies may be viewed by others. We may hide our bodies through baggy clothes, or make excuses rather than get together with a friend we haven't seen in years. If the choice is between not seeing our old friend or risking looking older or less attractive, we might pick the former. Experts estimate that as many as 10 percent of us restrict our lives because we are so self-conscious about some aspect of our looks.

Whether we put tremendous energy into self-improvement or we channel our efforts into avoiding threatening situations (or some combination of the two), the intent is self-protection. When we are insecure about our appearance, it makes sense that we would work hard to minimize the risk that our painful feelings will surface.

Sometimes we may even use our appearance obsession to hide other problems. For example, if we feel out of control of our feelings in a relationship, we may try to take control of our bodies. It may feel safer to improve our appearance rather than address our fear of confronting someone or our terror over the thought that our significant other will find someone else.

One key to learning appearance security is to evaluate the impact of our behavior honestly. For example, if we avoid social situations because we don't have a new outfit or if we put off plans until we lose weight, we might protect ourselves from feelings of self-consciousness or fears of social judgment. Therefore, our intention may be to nurture and protect ourselves.

Yet the impact of this decision can be detrimental to our self-worth. First, we exclude ourselves from potentially enjoyable situations. Second, we don't give ourselves the opportunity to test the reality of our fears, or to rely on ourselves to live through and handle whatever situation arises. Third, we continue to give ourselves the message that the way others view us determines our value as a person or dictates our view of how attractive we feel.

BEHAVIOR STRATEGIES THAT WORK

Do not link your plans with your looks. If you tend to put off activities until you improve your appearance, make a promise to yourself to STOP! Develop a list of goals and activities that you've been delaying and set a schedule for doing them.

Tackle uncomfortable situations. When we find ourselves avoiding a situation, we need to examine closely what it is that we are afraid of. Most of the time we discover that what we are really afraid of is the painful messages that will surface if our worst fantasy comes true. For instance, if you avoid bathing suit shopping, you may think your worst fear is looking terrible or wearing a larger size than you think you "should." Maybe you're even afraid that you won't fit into one, or you anticipate a disapproving look from the salesperson.

While none of these events would be pleasant (who likes swimsuit shopping anyway?), they would certainly not be unbearable. However, if these possible worst-case scenarios would start an avalanche of self-criticism about your appearance, you might be a lot more motivated to avoid this activity. Yet it would be your own reaction to, and interpretation of, this event that would cause you the most trouble — not the event itself.

Using the following guidelines can help you replace fear and avoidance with confidence and more options to choose from.

Learn To Relax

It is important to realize that you will probably have some anxiety when you first approach an uncomfortable situation. Convincing yourself that you will branch out when you are less afraid of a situation is understandable; unfortunately, it doesn't usually work that way. However, learning relaxation techniques can be a good way to help you manage your anxiety and reduce the physical arousal that fear often generates. There are a number of excellent relaxation tapes on the market; the best strategy is to find one that appeals to you personally.

Take Control

Limit the time you will spend in the uncomfortable situation. Take a friend along. Plan a pleasurable activity afterward. In short, take control of as many aspects of the situation as you can, and structure it in a way that is best for you.

My friend with the swimsuit shopping anxiety has developed a plan of attack that works for her; she limits the number of suits she tries on, plans a pleasurable treat after she finishes and reminds herself of the joys of swimming before she goes. Focusing on the pleasures of swimming also helps her pay attention to the comfort and fit of the bathing suit (what it does) rather than the swimsuit size (or how she thinks she looks in it).

Put It In Perspective

What effect will the outcome of the frightening situation have on you five years from now? How would you feel if your imagined worst-case scenario happened to your best friend? Would it change the way you felt about her? What are the possible opportunities in the situation?

Focusing on the possible benefits and putting the potential negatives into perspective can help you prepare for a new or threatening situation. When I first started speaking in public, I used this strategy over and over again. While my anxiety did not go away until after I had spoken numerous times, putting my fears into perspective helped me get up in front of my first audiences. It also helped me see that the expectations and pressures I was putting on myself were certainly not the same ones I would put on a friend.

We can use the "perspective" approach to loosen the hold of appearance obsession in general. One of my clients made a list of role models, women whom she admired and aspired to emulate. She was gratified to realize that looks had nothing at all to do with many of her goals and aspirations. The women on her list came in all shapes and sizes, and she admired them for their attitudes, leadership and accomplishments.

A Final Thought About Body Image

While our cultural ideals set the stage for negative thoughts and feelings, the degree of importance we give them is closely related to our appearance satisfaction. These thoughts and feelings about our appearance affect not only our attitude toward ourselves, they may also influence how we act in many areas of our lives. They can prevent us from taking advantage of social opportunities, or they can lead us to focus on self-improvement rather than address underlying fears and concerns. Because our view of our appearance is closely linked with our value of ourselves, we can easily believe that improving our appearance satisfaction will solve other problems: however, the reverse is often true.

Throughout this book we have looked at the personal impact of our society's cultural beauty standards. We have seen how, as individuals, we have little direct control over cultural beauty messages even though we may feel their impact on a daily basis.

Are there things we can do to combat our society's appearance obsession? I believe the answer is yes. What can we do *now* to change our society's focus on looks? How can we prevent our children from developing eating disorders or abusing steroids? Turn to Chapter 11 for some answers.

BREAKING THE CYCLE: BEYOND OURSELVES

This book began with my personal history of appearance obsession. For many years I worked hard to achieve an "ideal" appearance. I religiously, and at times frantically, engaged in a variety of self-improvement strategies. I thought my goal was an improved appearance, but what I was really seeking was relief from the ongoing dissatisfaction and insecurity I felt about my looks. At the time I thought the two were the same — if I looked better, I would feel better.

My focus was on how to look better. There was, and is, plenty of available advice. Diet books crowd the bookstore shelves and virtually every current magazine has at least one article about exercise. Product advertisements urge us to buy a better look. Get the right hair replacement, the right outfit, build enough muscles through a new exercise machine, and we will someday obtain the ideal appearance — and as an added bonus, the new, improved lives that go with them!

During my struggle I often felt ashamed of the importance looks held in my life, yet I was afraid to change my behavior. If I felt dissatisfied with my looks in spite of my self-improvement regime, how would I feel if I gave it up? Fears of potential weight gain, of lost muscle tone or of looking older can be powerful motivators, at least for a while. Finally, however, I began to wonder why looks were so important to me and what I could do to change this.

Throughout this book we have seen how unrealistic these beauty programs are. We have replaced how-to beauty programs with an understanding of why these programs are important to so many of us. We have talked about what we can do to combat these, by recognizing them when they occur, by understanding our personal beauty history and by getting a balance between self-improvement and self-acceptance.

Once we feel secure about our own appearance, we can do something to change our society's appearance obsession. Parents often ask me what they can do to promote their child's body image. They express concern about the increasing prevalence of eating disorders, the mental illness with the highest mortality rate. Prejudice against obesity is rampant in our culture, yet only two states have laws that forbid discrimination based on body size. This chapter will explore some specific ways we can fight our society's obsession with looks.

Challenging Our Society's Appearance Obsession

"Fatism" — discrimination based on body size — starts early. Children develop an active dislike of obesity by age six. By age seven they have acquired "ideal" perceptions of attractiveness. By age ten our prejudice against obesity is firmly in place. Because these attitudes are based on our culture's values and priorities, and therefore determine what is socially acceptable, we may be completely unaware of their influence. Yet, if not challenged, they are likely to influence our adult ways of thinking and acting directly. We must unlearn them before we can learn something new.

As adults, one of the hardest things to unlearn in our culture is the prejudice we have against people who are overweight. Credentials being equal, overweight people are discriminated against in the job market and the college admission process. They have a harder time obtaining housing. These alarming statistics tell us that fatism is prevalent; however, looking at one person's experiences awakens us to the personal devastation that fatism creates.

LEE'S STORY

Lee responded to an ad I placed in the *Dallas Observer* asking readers to write to me about the personal impact of our society's emphasis on looks. With her permission, here are some excerpts from her letter:

"I am a fat woman. I do not say that in an apologetic tone, it is merely a description, a perfectly good word that allows me to quickly convey a number of facts. I am 5'2", very rounded and generously proportioned. I cannot tell you how much I weigh, as I have not owned a bathroom scale in the ten years since I decided there were worse things than being fat — such as being dead.

"Society and a 33 billion-dollar-a-year diet industry tell you that being slim makes you look good. Between the ages of 8 and 30, I believed them. Counting back from the time my mother put me on a diet at age eight, through my doctor's prescription of amphetamines at age 15, until I realized at age 30 that I was a beautiful and worthwhile person despite my being built like a fat woman, I lost in excess of 1,000 pounds. And gained it back. I was willing for a while to put up with feeling bad, malnutrition, stressing my body with constant and sizeable weight changes, even risking death trying to reach our society's image of what a woman was supposed to look like."

Lee goes on to share many painful memories. From repeatedly cruel comments from strangers, to exploitive marketing approaches by employees of the diet industry (you have such a pretty face), to a woman calling her a "pig" and throwing a drink on her at a bar, she describes the personal agony she has endured over the past 20 years — all because of her body size.

As we can see from her letter, at age 30 Lee gave up dieting and learned to accept her natural body size. Today Lee seems to be at peace with her looks. Unfortunately, however, the discrimination continues. Lee went on to say that as she began to accept her body size, societal pressure got worse. In her words, "At least when you're overweight and on a diet, people can see that you're doing something about it." How often do we give these same messages to ourselves?

Adjusting Our Attitude

As we saw in Chapter 9, we all make assumptions about people based on how they look. Becoming aware of our prejudices and working to get past them gives us the opportunity to get to know the person inside. On a more personal level, the attitudes we have toward others often mirror the expectations and judgments we place on ourselves.

For instance, we now know that our weight is determined by a number of factors, some of which are out of our control. New research is continuing to add to the body of evidence that points to heredity and genetics as major weight influences. If we persist in telling ourselves that we do have total control over our own weight, we are also blaming ourselves when we fail to lose it. Taking this one step further, not only will we hold ourselves accountable for our weight, we will also judge other people by their body size.

The link between our attitudes toward our own looks and fatism is even more direct. Studies indicate that people who view themselves as relatively lean (or at least lean enough) make fewer judgments toward obese men and women. If we are accepting of our own body size, we are less judgmental of others. This is especially true for women who, because of the strong cultural mandates to be thin, tend to be more critical of others who are overweight.

The Other Side Of Looks Prejudice

Believe it or not, even beauty can be a burden. In Chapter 8, we looked at the pros and cons of physical attractiveness. Looking good entails certain social advantages, but it also has drawbacks. Beautiful people often feel tremendous public pressure and are frequently self-conscious about how they are coming across to others. Extremely attractive people often cite a "beauty is vanity" prejudice. Many people feel threatened or resentful of extremely good-looking people and reject them out of hand.

When talking about her beauty, Candice Bergen once said, "People see you as an object, not a person, and they project a set of expectations on you. People who don't have it think beauty is a blessing, but actually it sets you apart." No one wins when we make assumptions based solely on appearance.

Helping Our Daughters

Some studies indicate that up to 25 percent of seven-year-old girls have attempted to lose weight. Along with the normal physical changes of puberty, we see a rise in depression and a poor body image emerge among teenage girls. Most eating disorders begin between the ages of 9 and 11, yet there are no available eating-disorder prevention programs that target this age group. Our culture's beauty messages are taking their toll not only on us but also on our daughters.

As parents (or future parents), we cannot directly control the media or prevent the peer pressure our daughters will inevitably feel about their looks. Following are some things we *can* do.

Role Model Appearance Security

Our children will do what we do, not what we tell them to do. Learning to put our own looks in perspective is the most important thing we can do to combat society's impact on our children. Parents who feel good about themselves and who place an emphasis on health and emotional well-being give their children an edge. Learning appearance security is an ongoing process; we should strive for progress, not perfection. We can start to model this for our children by:

- eating naturally
- exercising together — and for fun
- forbidding sibling teasing, particularly about looks
- watching our comments about the appearance of others
- showing love through attention, not through purchases
- stopping our diets

Teach Your Child To View Media Messages With A Critical Eye

While we cannot protect our daughters from exposure to our culture's beauty ideals, we can help put them in perspective. We can help them see the relative nature of beauty and how we learn what is considered culturally beautiful. This is particularly helpful when the girls are between the ages of 9 and 11, before they reach puberty. Here are some ways we can help them learn to put beauty messages in perspective.

A. Expose your child to beauty ideals in other countries. Teach her about beauty standards that have appeared during different periods in history. As you read about these together, talk about the painful (and often dangerous) consequences of various "beauty-enhancing" procedures in different cultures, and compare these to our society's preoccupation with dieting and plastic surgery. Seeing the crippling effects of China's historical foot-binding procedures, for instance, will help her understand the subjective nature of ideal beauty and the risks of trying to meet it.

B. Look at your child's favorite magazines with her. Point out the beauty messages you encounter. Talk about the models and compare them to the body sizes of most people she knows. Count the number of diet and exercise articles you find and talk about the looks messages they send to the readers.

C. Take her to Glamour Shots. Glamour Shots is a national photography chain that is very popular with teenage girls partly because of the glamourous photographs they produce. As part of their photography they include hair and makeup consultation before the picture is taken. They also use special lighting. Seeing the dramatic effects of cosmetics and lighting on herself can help your daughter see her favorite magazine models in a new, more realistic light.

Respect Your Child's Eating And Accept Her Body Size

Regardless of your child's body size, attempting to control your child's eating does more harm than good. As parents we have a right to determine when our family eats and what food will be served. Our children have the right to determine how much they will eat.

While our motivation may be to help her fight family genetics, or to prevent painful teasing, the results of trying to control your child's eating will be increased self-consciousness, difficulty trusting herself to regulate her own eating and family turmoil. In addition, studies suggest that because of the physical changes that accompany adolescence, teenage dieting may actually result in more difficulties with weight control as an adult.

Establish A Good Communication Pattern

Many parents express concern when they hear their daughter talking negatively about her appearance, or when she suddenly goes on a diet. Unfortunately, these are normal activities for teenage girls. The best response is often to listen and to ask what she is unhappy about or why she thinks a diet is important. Responding to your daughter's feelings and letting her know that you think she looks fine will reassure her that you understand her perspective and that you are proud of her just the way she is.

If you find laxatives or diet pills in your daughter's possession, don't panic. DO talk immediately with your daughter and express your concern. Read the information below; this information will help you know if and when you need to seek professional help.

Stay Informed

Because of the shame and concern many of us feel about our weight and our appearance, people who develop eating disorders often go to great lengths to hide it from others. As parents our role is to be aware of red flags, not to diagnose. If you observe any of the following behaviors, it is time to seek medical consultation:

- Your daughter expresses extreme fear of being fat when she is of normal weight or below normal weight.
- Your daughter consistently heads for the bathroom immediately after meals.
- Your daughter exercises to the point that it is interfering with her school work or social life.
- Your daughter continues to diet even when she begins to get feedback from others that she is too thin.
- You discover laxatives, diet pills or diuretics on more than one occasion.

- You consistently find empty food wrappers hidden in private places, such as under her bed or in her car.
- Your daughter develops an extreme interest in food but only eats very small portions.

Fight Weight Or Appearance Criteria In School Activities

Until very recently, several Dallas high schools had strict weight restrictions, assessed height-to-weight ratios and often conducted fat analyses on cheerleaders and drill team members. Is it any wonder that many of the girls developed signs of eating disorders? The good news — these measures were recently dropped as a result of strong protests by concerned parents and professionals. Weight or appearance pressures are all too common in many of the activities in which girls participate. Find out if these are present in your daughter's school and lobby to erase them.

Promote Eating-Disorder Prevention Programs

Many schools provide education about health and nutrition. These programs often include information about the medical risks that have been associated with obesity. While this is important information, it is equally important to balance this information with education about the risks of dieting and eating disorders. Without it, we run the risk of substituting one potential health problem for another.

HELPING OUR SONS

As we saw in Chapter 6, looks and performance can be closely related for boys. Looking masculine and being strong often go together. Among high school steroid users, the number-one reason for drug use was to enhance their performance; the second reason was to "improve" their looks. This was especially true when it came to athletic participation.

Just as our daughters are exposed to models and beauty contests, our sons can't help but notice the attention given to sports celebrities. They most likely will encounter coaches who have a "winning is everything" mentality. They will inevitably observe the popularity and favoritism often accorded high school and college athletes.

Taken to the extreme, these pressures concerning athletic performance can distort our sons' priorities. Consider this: in a study of 100 junior world class athletes (ages 19 and under), 70 percent said that they would take a "magic pill" that would bring them a gold medal even if they would die after five years. While our sons might not be Olympic athletes, performance pressures can lead to poor choices — including steroid abuse.

ROCKY'S STORY

Norman "Rocky" Rauch is the most remarkable person I have encountered during my research for this book. Holding down a full-time job and recovering from his third bout with cancer (which he believes to be a direct result of steroid abuse), he travels from high school to high school warning students about steroid use. His story illustrates the pressures many of our sons face and what we can do about them.

Rocky began weightlifting in high school after he was beaten up by two boys. He describes his initial motivation as a "revenge thing." In two years, training two hours a day for six days a week, he went from 135 pounds to 255 pounds — without using steroids. He began competitive weightlifting after he enlisted in the Air Force, and in 1964 he qualified for the Olympic tryouts. Without steroids. The accomplishments Rocky achieved *without* using steroids are a major focus in his talks with high school and college students. Rocky is aware of the performance pressures many athletes are under as well as their fear that they will be unable to compete athletically without taking steroids.

Rocky unknowingly began using steroids after they were prescribed by an Olympic physician in 1968. In 1971 he developed boils and discovered he had a damaged immune system and a deteriorated liver. He also discovered that the pills he had been taking were steroids. While his condition improved after 30 days off steroids, Rocky's desire to excel at weightlifting eventually overcame his health concerns. He began taking steroids voluntarily.

In 1986, he was diagnosed with non-Hodgkin's lymphoma. Rocky talks matter-of-factly about his history of steroid abuse. He vividly describes his extreme mood swings, which he believes led to the breakup of three marriages. Even today, although he has been cancer-free for over three years, he continues to suffer from a variety of medical problems.

STEROID ABUSE: HOW PARENTS CAN REDUCE THE RISK

Set An Example

If we use drugs or alcohol to cope with our insecurities or our daily pressures, it may be an easier choice for our teenagers to choose drugs as an aid to enhance their athletic performance or to feel more secure about their identities or looks.

Keep Sports In Perspective

One of the biggest challenges of parenting is separating our own ambitions and desires from our children's natural interests and abilities. Fathers who can follow their son's lead regarding sports participation, and who can be supportive no matter how their child performs, can make great strides in offsetting performance pressures from other sources.

Stay Informed

Get to know your son's coaches. Many exceptional coaches work hard to use sports in a positive manner. Here's one example: A client recently told me that her ten-year-old son often came home crying because his peers frequently teased him about his small size, often calling him "skinny" and "shrimp." His physical education coach, noting this, gave a brief talk to the class about the advantages of different body sizes in different sports. Among his examples, he specifically mentioned this boy's "lean" build and talked about the quickness that often comes with a small frame. The teasing stopped and the boy came home glowing with pride.

On the other hand, coaches who are highly critical of their players or who ignore injuries in order to win have no place in sports.

Get Involved At School

Because of the high incidence of steroid use among serious high school and college athletes, Rocky staunchly advocates intermittent drug testing at the high school and college level. Testing that is approved by the International Olympic Council and that is administered by an outside party (not monitored by the school's athletic department) is ideal. Find out if random drug testing is routinely conducted if your son is involved in a college athletic program. If not, advocate it.

QUESTIONS PARENTS ASK

What Is The Relationship Between Dieting And Eating Disorders?

There is definitely a link between dieting and eating disorders. While most eating disorders begin with dieting, most girls who diet do not develop an eating disorder. More and more of the research suggests that dieting plus depression is the key. That is, girls who are depressed and begin dieting are at the greatest risk of developing an eating disorder.

My Teenager Wants Plastic Surgery. What Should I Do?

While I personally believe that all aesthetic cosmetic surgery decisions should be made after age 18, other experts disagree. The American Society of Aesthetic Plastic Surgery and The American Society for Plastic and Reconstructive Surgery suggests the following guidelines:

- The teenager, not the parent, should always be the one to voice the desire for plastic surgery.
- The request should be expressed more than once and over a period of time.
- Breast enlargement, liposuction and cheek implants are not recommended for teenagers.
- The teenager's reasons for and expectations of plastic surgery should be carefully evaluated.
- Teenagers who change their dress style, hair color or other aspects of their appearance regularly are often not good candidates for plastic surgery.

It is particularly important to find out how long your child has been unhappy with a particular feature, what exactly it is that he or she doesn't like and how he or she thinks plastic surgery will change his or her life. If he or she is attributing a lack of popularity or a relationship breakup to a less-than-perfect facial feature, plastic surgery is not the answer.

What Should I Do If I Think My Son Is Taking Steroids?

Some of the signs of steroid use include rapid weight gain (for example, gaining 30 pounds in three months), severe mood swings, an increase in aggressive behavior and hair loss. If you see these signs in your son, confront him. If he admits that he is using steroids, seek medical advice to help him quit and to assist him with withdrawal symptoms.

If he denies it, ask him to take a drug test. While this may seem like a hard line to take, most professionals agree that denial is the most common response. If he agrees, then the drug test will either confirm or relieve your suspicions. If he refuses, you have your answer already and should immediately seek medical assistance.

A Final Thought About Appearance Obsession

Combating society's obsession with looks starts with each of us taking a close look at how we feel about our own appearances and evaluating how these feelings affect our behavior, our relationships and our lives. It continues when we decide to take a stand and set our own beauty standards.

Once we feel secure about the way we look and have developed a self-determined balance between self-improvement and self-acceptance, there is a lot more we can do. We can work to fight discrimination based on looks or size. We can channel our energy into promoting school education about eating disorders or steroid abuse. We can focus on eliminating family appearance pressures. We can help kids build body images by working as volunteer coaches or as club leaders.

Pick an area that touches you, one that you feel strongly about. Commit to an effort that you will enjoy, one that will be personally rewarding to you. Once you decide, do it.

Ultimately, the most important relationship we have is the one between ourselves and our reflection in the mirror. It is through this relationship that we define and affirm who we are. May your mirror increasingly recognize your true value, and may your reflection show an increasing contentment with your looks.

ENDNOTES

2. Are You Appearance Obsessed?

Page Number

19   Shapiro, L. and Leonard, E. A. "Everybody's Got A Hungry Heart." *Newsweek* (May 13, 1991) 58-59.

19   1986 Study by Lauren Millin cited in "A Better Body Image," Ressler, A.; Randall, L. *WW Magazine,* July 1991, p. 54, 56.

19   "Everybody's Got A Hungry Heart." See pg. 219 of references.

19   1990 Statistics provided by the American Society for Plastic and Reconstructive Surgery.

20   Rodin, J., Silberstein, L. and Striegel-Moore, R. "Women and Weight: A Normative Discontent." In *Nebraska Symposium on Motivation* 32 (1985): 267-307.

21   McCarthy, M. "The Thin Ideal and Eating Disorders in Women." *Behavior Research Therapy* 28, no. 3 (1990): 205-215.

21   Nolen-Hoeksema, S. "Sex Differences in Unipolar Depression: Evidence and Theory." *Psychological Bulletin* 101 (1987): 259-289.

21   Nasser, M. "Comparative Study of the Prevalence of Abnormal Eating Attitudes Among Arab Female Students of Both London and Cairo University." *Psychological Medicine* 16 (1986): 621-625.

21   Silber, T. "Anorexia Nervosa in Blacks and Hispanics." *International Journal of Eating Disorders* 5 (1986): 121-128.

21   Thomas, J. P. and Szmulker, G. I. "Anorexia Nervosa in Patients of Afro-Caribbean Extraction." *British Journal of Psychiatry* 146 (1985): 653-656.

21   Silverstein, B., Peterson, B. and Perdue, L. "Some Correlates of the Thin Standard of Bodily Attractiveness for Women." *International Journal of Eating Disorders* 5, no. 5 (1986): 895-905.

27   Lerner, R. M.; Iwasaki, S., Chihara, T. and Sorrell, G. T. "Self-Concept, Self-Esteem, and Body Attitudes Among Japanese Male and Female Adolescents," in S. Chess and A. Thomas, eds. *Annual Progress in Child Psychiatry and Child Development.* New York: Bruner/Mazel, Inc., 1981, 495-507.

3. The Beauty Culture Club

35   "Find Young Girls Starving To Keep Overweight," quote given by Ms. Emma Holloway, Supervisor of the Institutional and Dietetic Courses at Pratt Institute, at the Ninth Annual American Dietetic Association Convention. *New York Times* (October 12, 1926): 13.

36   Kaiser, S. *The Social Psychology of Clothing: Symbolic Appearances in Context.* New York: Macmillan Publishing Company, 1990, 109-115.

39   *Dick and Jane as Victims: Sex Stereotyping in Children's Readers.* Available from Women on Words and Images, Box 2163, Princeton, NJ 08540.

39   Silverstein, B., Perdue, L., Peterson, B. and Kelly, E. "The Role of the Mass Media in Promoting a Thin Standard of Bodily Attractiveness." *Women's Sex Roles* 14 (1986): 519-532.

39   Wiseman, C., Gray, J., Mosimann, J. and Ahrens, A. "Cultural Expectations of Thinness in Women: An Update." *International Journal of Eating Disorders* 11, no. 1 (1992): 85-89.

39   Downs, C. A. and Harrison, S. K. "Embarrassing Age Spots or Just Plain Ugly? Physical Attractiveness Stereotyping as an Instrument of Sexism on American Television Commericials." *Sex Roles* 13 (1985): 9-19.

39   Stewart, D. "In the Cutthroat World of Toy Sales, Child's Play Is Serious Business." *Smithsonian* (December) (1989): 73-83.

39   Evans, E. D., Ruthberg, J., Sather, C. and Turner, C. *Content Analysis of Contemporary Teen Magazines*. Unpublished manuscript.

39   Nichter, M. and Nichter, M. "Hype and Weight." Medical Anthropology 13 (1991): 249-284.

39   Thompson, J. K. "Larger Than Life." *Psychology Today* 70 (1986): 38-39, 42, 44.

39   1992 statistics provided by the National Association of Anorexia Nervosa and Associated Eating Disorders.

39   Moses, N., Banilivy, M. and Lifshitz, F. "Fear of Obesity Among Adolescent Girls." *Pediatrics* 83: 393-398.

39   Wooley, S. C. and Wooley, O. W. "Feeling Fat In a Thin Society." *Glamour* (February, 1984): 198-252.

39   Dolan, B. M., Birtchnell, S. A. and Lacy, J. H. "Body Image Distortion in Non-Eating Disordered Women and Men." *Journal of Psychosomatic Research* 31, no. 4 (1987): 513-520.

40   Anderson, A. E. "Diet v. Shape Content of Popular Media and Female Magazines: A Dose-Response Relationship to the Incidence of Eating Disorders." *International Journal of Eating Disorders* 11, no. 3 (April 1992): 283-297.

40   Myers, P. and Biocca, F. "The Elastic Body Image: The Effects of Television Advertising and Programming on Body Image Distortions in Young Women." *Journal of Communication* 42, no. 3 (Summer 1992): 108-133.

41   Abramson, E. E. and Valene, P. "Media Use, Dietary Restraint, Bulimia, and Attitudes Toward Obesity: A Preliminary Study." *British Review of Bulimia and Anorexia Nervosa* 5, no. 2 (July 1991): 73-76.

42   Cash, T. F., Winstead, B. A. and Janda, L. H. "The Great American Shape-Up: We're Healthier Than Ever, Fitter Than Ever . . . But Less Satisfied With How We Look." *Psychology Today* 20, no. 4 (1986): 30-37.

42   Hey, B. "Portrait of An Obsession: America's Preoccupation With Beauty Won't Go Away." *Health* (June 1991): 68-71.

42   Mishkind, M. C., Rodin, J., Silberstein, L. and Striegel-Moore, R. H. "The Embodiment of Masculinity." *American Behavioral Scientist* 26, no. 5 (May/June 1986): 545-562.

42 Drewnowski, A. and Yee, D. K. "Men and Body Image: Are Men Satisfied With Their Body Weight?" *Psychosomatic Medicine* 49 (1987): 626-634.

43 Designer Lowell Nesbitt, quoted in article by Elizabeth Snead, "Macho Mannequins Muscle into Stores." *USA Today* (June 18, 1990: D1.

43 Anderson. "Diet v. Shape Content of Popular Media." *Op. cit.*

Snead. "Macho Mannequins Muscle into Stores." *Op. cit.*

43 "Men Just Don't Care." In the column "The Guy Thing." *U.S. News and World Report* 112, no. 4 (Feb. 3, 1992): 57(1).

43 Squires, S. "Which Diets Work?" *Working Woman* 17, no. 10: 92(2).

Mishkina, *et al.* "The Embodiment of Masculinity." *Op. cit.*

43 Tucker, L. A. "Relationship Between Perceived Somatotype and Body Cathexis on the Self-Concept of College Males." *Psychological Reports* 50 (1982): 983-989.

43 Hey. "Preoccupation with Beauty Won't Go Away." *Op. cit.*

43 Mishra, R. "Steroids and Sports Are a Losing Proposition." *FDA Consumer* (September 1991): 25-27.

43 Yoffa, E. "Valley of the Silicone Dolls" *Newsweek* (November 26, 1990): 72.

43 Troiano, L. "Reshaping Images: More Men Opt for Plastic Surgery." *American Health* (September 1990): 14.

43 Interview with Edward Spauster, Ph.D., Director of the Behavioral Disorders Unit at Holliswood Hospital. In Kabtznick, R. "True Reflections." *Weight Watcher's Magazine* 22 (June 1990): 24-25.

44 Statistic quoted in *Vitality Magazine* (March 1993): 16. Original source: First For Women, 270 Sylvan Avenue, P.O. Box 1649, Englewood Cliffs, NJ 07632.

4. Setting The Stage: Family Beauty Messages

52 Kaschak, E. *Engendered Lives: A New Psychology of Women's Experiences.* New York: Basic Books (HarperCollins Publisher), 1992.

52 Musa, K. and Roach, M. "Adolescent Appearance and Self-Concept." *Adolescence* 8 (1973): 385-394.

53 Fallon, A. E. and Rozin, P. "Sex Differences in Perceptions of Body Shape." *Journal of Abnormal Psychology* 94 (1985): 102-105.

54 Tannen, D. *You Just Don't Understand: Women and Men in Conversation.* New York: Ballantine Books, 1990.

54 McGuire, W. J. and McGuire, C. V. "Significant Others in Self-Space: Sex Differences and Developmental Trends in the Social Self." In J. Suls, ed. *Social Psychological Perspectives on the Self.* Hillsdale, NJ: Erlbaum, 1982, 71-96.

54 Chadorow, N. *The Reproduction of Mothering: Psychoanalysis and the Sociology of Gender.* Berkeley: University of California Press, 1978.

57 Striegel-Moore, R., Silberstein, L. and Rodin, J. "Toward An Understanding of the Risk Factors For Bulimia." *American Psychologist* 41, no. 3 (1986): 246-263.

58 Constanzo, P. R. and Woody, E. Z. "Domain-Specific Parenting Styles and Their Impact in the Child's Development of Particular Deviance: The Example of Obesity Proneness." *Journal of Social and Clinical Psychology* 3 (1985): 425-445.

59 Pike, K. and Rodin, J. "Mothers, Daughters and Disordered Eating." *Journal of Abnormal Psychology* 100, no. 2 (1991): 198-204.

59 Striegel-Moore, *et al.* "Toward an Understanding of the Risk Factors for Bulimia." *Op. cit.*

59 Nichter and Nichter. "Hype and Weight." *Op. cit.*, Endnotes, Chapter 3.

61 Suleiman, S. R. *The Female Body in Western Culture: Comtemporary Perspectives.* Cambridge: Harvard University Press, 1986.

61 Kaschak. *Engendered Lives. Op. cit.*

61 Brooks-Gunn, J. and Mathews, W. S. *He and She: How Children Develop Their Sex Role Identity.* Englewood Cliffs, NJ: Prentice-Hall, 1979, 72.

62 Kabatznick, R. "True Reflections." *Weight Watcher's Magazine* 22 (June 1990): 24-25.

62 Ressler, A. and Randall, L. "A Better Body Image." *Working Woman's Magazine* (July 1991): 54, 56.

63 Crago, M., Yates, A., Beutler, L. E. and Arizmendi, T. J. "Height-Weight Ratios Among Female Athletes: Are Collegiate Ath-

letes the Precursors to an Anorexia Syndrome?" *International Journal of Eating Disorders* 4 (1985): 79-87.

63   Garner, D. M. and Garfinkel, P. E. "Sociocultural Factors in the Development of Anorexia Nervosa." *Psychological Medicine* 10: 647-656.

63   Yates, A. *Compulsive Exercise and the Eating Disorders: Toward an Integrated Theory of Activity.* New York: Brunner/Mazel, 1991.

63   Schwartzberg, N. "Do I Look Fat?" *Parents* (January 1990): 66-70.

63   Simmons, R. G., Blyth, D. A. and McKinney, K. L. "The Social and Psychological Effects of Puberty on White Females." In J. Brooks-Gunn and A. C. Peterson, eds. *Girls at Puberty.* New York: Plenum Press, 1983.

63   Tobin-Richards, M. H., Boxer, A. M. and Peterson, A. C. Contributors to Brooks-Gunn and Peterson, *Girls At Puberty*, 127-154.

65   *Ibid.*

65   Clausen, J. A. "The Social Meaning of Differential Physical and Sexual Maturation." In S. E. Dragastin and G. H. Elders, Jr., eds. *Adolescence in the Life Cycle: Psychological Change and Social Context.* Washington, D.C.: Hemisphere, 1975, 24-48.

5. Dieting: Riding The Train To The Thin Farm

74   Pyle, R. L., Neuman, P. A., Halvorson, P. A. and Mitchell, J. A. "An Ongoing Cross-Sectional Study of the Prevalence of Eating Disorders in Freshman College Students." *International Journal of Eating Disorders* (November 1991): 667-677.

74   Rodin. "Women and Weight: A Normative Discontent." *Op. cit.,* Endnotes, Chapter 2.

75   Polivy, J. and Herman, C. P. *Breaking the Diet Habit: The Natural Weight Alternative.* New York: Basic Books, 1983.

77   Nisbett, R. E. "Eating Behavior and Obesity in Man and Animals." *Advances in Psychosomatic Medicine* 7 (1972): 173-193.

78   Schelkun, P. H. "The Risks of Riding the Weight Loss Rollercoaster." *The Physician and Sportsmedicine* 19, no. 6 (June 1991): 149-156.

81   Herman, C. P. and Mack, D. "Restrained and Unrestrained Eating." *Journal of Personality* 43 (1979): 647-660.

82   Baucom, D. H. and Aiken, P. A. "Effect of Depressed Mood on Eating Among Obese and Nonobese Dieting and Nondieting Persons." *Journal of Personality and Social Psychology* 41 (1981): 577-588.

82   Polivy, J. and Herman, C. P. "Effects of Alcohol Consumption on Eating Behavior: Influences of Mood and Perceived Intoxication." *Journal of Abnormal Psychology* 85: 601-606.

82   Schotte, D. E., Cools, J. and McNally, R. J. "Induced Anxiety Triggers Overeating." *Journal of Abnormal Psychology* 99 (1990): 317-320.

84   Polivy, J. and Herman, C. P. "Dieting and Binging: A Causal Analysis." *American Psychologist* 40 (1985): 193-201.

84   Polivy, J. and Herman, C. P. "Diagnosis and Treatment of Normal Eating." *Journal of Consulting and Clinical Psychology* 55 (1987): 635-644.

84   Halmi, K. A. and Schwartz, E. "Binge Eating and Vomiting: A Survey of a College Population." *Psychological Medicine* 11 (1981): 697-706.

84   Hawkins, R. C. and Clement, P. F. "Development and Construct Validity of a Self-Report Measure of Binge Eating Tendencies." *Addictive Behaviors* 5 (1980): 219-226.

84   Olmstead, M. P. and Garner, D. M. "The Significance of Self-Induced Vomiting As a Weight Control Method Among College Women." Unpublished manuscript, Clarke Institute of Psychiatry, Toronto, Canada.

84   O'Neill, M. "A Growing Movement Fights Diets Instead of Fat." *The New York Times National* (April 12, 1992): 41.

85   Toufexis, A. "Forget About Losing Those Last Ten Pounds." *Time* (July 8, 1991): 50-51.

85   Quote from Dr. Kelly Brownell, cited in *ibid.*

85   Rosenthal, E. "Commercial Diets Lack Proof of Their Long-Term Success." *The New York Times* (November 24, 1992): A1, LC11.

85   Calloway, W. *The Calloway Diet.* New York: Bantam Books, Inc., 1990.

85   Contreras, R. J. and Williams, V. L. "Dietary Obesity and Weight Cycling: Effects on Blood Pressure and Heart Rate in Rats."

American Journal of Physiology 256, no. 6, pt. 2 (1989): R1209-R1212.

85   Kern, P. A., Ong, J., Saffari, *et al.* "The Effects of Weight Loss on the Activity and Expression of Adipose Tissue Lipoprotein Lipase in Very Obese Humans." *New England Journal of Medicine* 322, no. 15, (1990): 1053-1059.

85   Klesges, R. C., Klem, M. L. and Epkins, C. C. "A Longitudinal Evaluation of Dietary Restraint and Its Relationship to Changes in Body Weight." *Addictive Behaviors* 16 (1991): 363-368.

91   Revised weight tables issued by the U.S. Department of Agriculture and the Department of Health and Human Services, 1990.

93   O'Neill, M. "A Growing Movement Fights Diets Instead of Fat." *The New York Times National* (April 12, 1992): L41-L42.

93   Wooley, S. C. and Wooley, O. W. "Intensive Outpatient and Residential Treatment for Bulimia." In D. M. Garner and P. E. Garfinkel, eds. *Handbook of Psychotherapy for Anorexia and Bulimia.* New York: Guilford Press, 1985.

94   Silverstein, B., Peterson, B., and Perdue, L. "Some Correlates of the Thin Standard of Bodily Attractiveness for Women." *International Journal of Eating Disorders* 5, no. 5 (1986): 895-905.

94   McCarthy, M. "The Thin Ideal, Depression, and Eating Disorders in Women." *Behavior Research Therapy* 28, no. 3 (1990): 205-215.

6. Exercising To Look Good

98   MacMillan, J. "No Pain and Lots of Gain." *U.S. News and World Report* (May 1, 1992): 86, 88.

98   "Physical Activity and Psychological Benefits: The International Society of Sports Psychology Position Statement." *The Physician and Sportsmedicine* 20, no. 10 (October 1992): 179-184.

98   Rodin, J. and Plante, T. G. "The Psychological Effects of Exercise." In R. S. Williams and A. Wallace, eds. *Biological Effects of Physical Activity.* Champaign, IL: Human Kinetics Books, 1989, 127-137.

99   Neiman, D. C. "Exercise: How Much is Enough? How Much is Too Much?" *Women's Sports and Fitness* (June 1989): 31.

99 Stephens, T. "Physical Activity and Mental Health in the United States and Canada: Evidence From Four Population Surveys." *Preventative Medicine* 17, no. 1 (1988): 35-47.

99 *Ibid.*

99 Petruzello, S. J., Landers, D. M., Hatfield, B. D., *et al.* "A Meta-Analysis on the Anxiety-Reducing Effects of Acute and Chronic Exercise: Outcomes and Mechanisms." *Sports Medicine* 11, no. 3 (1991): 143-182.

99 Crews, D. J. and Landers, D. M. "A Meta-Analytic Review of Aerobic Fitness and Reactivity to Psychosocial Stressors." *Medical Science Sports Medicine* 19 (1987): S114-S120.

99 Dunn, A. L. and Dishman, R. K. "Exercise and the Neurobiology of Depression." *Exercise Sport Science Review* 19 (1991) 41-98.

99 Martinsen, E. W. "Interaction of Exercise and Medication in the Psychiatry Patient." In W. P. Morgan and S. E. Goldston, eds. *Exercise and Mental Health.* Washington, D.C.: Hemisphere Publishing Corp., 1987, 85-95.

99 North, T. C., McCullagh, P. and Tran, Z. V. "Effect of Exercise on Depression." *Exercise Sport Science Review* 18 (1990): 379-415.

100 Mole, P. A., Stern, J. S., Schultz, C. L., *et. al.* "Exercise Reverses Depressed Metabolic Rate Produced by Severe Caloric Restriction." *Medicine and Science in Sports and Exercise* 21 (1989): 29-35.

100 Kayman, S., Bruwold, W. and Stern, J. S. "Maintenance and Relapse After Weight Loss in Women." *American Journal of Clinical Nutrition* (1992) in press.

101 Nieman. "Exercise: How Much is Enough?"

101 McMahon, L. F., Ryan, M. J., Larsson, D., *et al.* "Occult Gastrointestinal Blood Loss in Marathon Runners." *Annals of Internal Medicine* 100 (1984): 846-847.

101 Barrow, G. W. and Saha, S. "Menstrual Irregularity and Stress Fractures in Collegiate Female Distance Runners." *American Journal of Sports Medicine* 16 (1988): 209-215.

101 Interview with Michael L. Pollock, Ph.D., professor of medicine at the University of Florida in Gainesville. In DeBenedette, V. "Are Your Patients Exercising Too Much?" *The Physician and Sportsmedicine* 18, no. 8: 119, 122.

102   Brownell, K. D., Rodin, J. and Wilmore, J. "National Runners Sur-
       vey on Dieting and Stress." *Runner's World* (August 1988): 32.

102   Short, S. M. and Short, W. R. "Four Year Study of University
       Athletes' Dietary Intake." *Journal of the American Dietetic Associ-
       ation* 82 (1989): 632-645.

102   Drinkwater, B. L., Nilson, K., Chestnut, C. M., *et al.* "Bone Min-
       eral Content of Amenorrheic and Eunomenorrheic Athletes."
       New England Journal of Medicine 311 (1984): 277-281.

103   Brownell, K. D., Steen, S. N. and Wilmore, J. M. "Weight Regulation
       Practices in Athletes: Analysis of Metabolic and Health Effects."
       Medicine and Science in Sports and Exercise 19 (1987): 552-560.

103   Adame, D., Johnson, T., Cole, P., *et al.* "Physical Fitness in Relation
       to Amount of Physical Exercise, Body Image, and Locus of
       Control Among College Men and Women." *Perceptual and Motor
       Skills* 70 (1990): 1347-1350.

105   Kobb, K. "When Is Too Much of a Good Thing Bad?" *American
       Health* (October 1989): 83.

107   MacMillan. "No Pain and Lots of Gain."

107   Sheehan, G. "Striding in the Comfort Zone." *The Physician and
       Sportsmedicine* 19, no. 11 (November 1991): 53, no. 1.*

107   The American College of Sports Medicine. "The Recommended
       Quantity and Quality of Exercise for Developing and Main-
       taining Cardiorespiratory and Muscular Fitness in Healthy
       Adults." *Medical Science Sports Exercise* 22, no. 2 (1990): 265-274.

110   Wichmann, S. and Martin, D. R. "Exercise Excess: Treating Pa-
       tients Addicted to Fitness." *The Physician and Sportsmedicine* 20,
       no. 5 (May 1992): 193-196, 199-200.

111   Thune, J. "Personality of Weight Lifters." *Research Quarterly of the
       American Physical Education Association* 20 (1949): 296-306.

111   Harlow, R. "Masculine Inadequacy and the Compensatory Devel-
       opment of Physique." *Journal of Personality* 19 (1951): 312-333.

112   Miskkind, M., Rodin, J., Silberstein, L. and Striegel-Moore, R.
       "The Embodiment of Masculinity: Cultural, Psychological, and
       Behavioral Dimensions." *American Behavioral Scientist* 29, no. 5
       (May/June, 1986): 545-562.

---

* See also Mishra. "Steroids and Sports Are a Losing Proposition." Endnotes, Chapter 3.

112 Fultz, O. "Roid Rage." *American Health* 60 (May 1991): 60, 62-64.

112 1987 survey of 3,400 12th grade boys cited in *Ibid*.

112 Todd, T. "The Steroid Predicament." *Sports Illustrated* 59, issue 5 (August 1, 1983): 65-74.*

*113 Kibble, M. and Ross, M. September 1987 article in *Clinical Psychopharmacology* cited in Roger Miller. "Athletes and Steroids: Playing a Deadly Game." *FDA Consumer* (November 18, 1987): 17-21.*

113 *Ibid.*

113 Miller. "Athletes and Steroids."

113 "Teenagers Blase About Steroid Abuse." "Updates" column. *FDA Consumer* (December 2, 1990): 2, 3.

113 *Ibid.*

113 Fultz. *Roid Rage.* New steroid estimates, check Chapter 3.

113 Miller. "Athletes and Steroids." *Op.cit.*

7. When Clothes Hide Too Much

118 Arthur, C. "Fifteen Million Americans Are Shopping Addicts." *American Demographics* 14, no. 3 (March, 1992): 14, no. 2.

118 Krier, B. A. "Can Retail Therapy Cure the Blues?" *Los Angeles Times* 110 (November 1, 1991): E1.

119 Virginia Slims poll conducted by the Roper organization, cited *Ibid*.

120 Lesser, J. A. and Kamal, P. "An Inductively Derived Model of the Motivation to Shop." *Psychology and Marketing* 8, no. 3 (Fall 1991): 177-196.

120 Markee, N., Carey, I. and Pederson, E. L. "Body Cathexis and Clothes Cathexis: Is There a Difference?" *Perceptual and Motor Skills* 70 (1990): 1239-1244.

120 Tyrchniewicz, M. E. and Gonzales, C. A. "The Relationship Between Specific Clothing Variables and Self-Concept of Adult Women." *Canadian Home Economics Journal* 28, no. 3 (1978): 189-196.

---

* See also Mishra. "Steroids and Sports Are a Losing Proposition." Endnotes, Chapter 3.

120   Faber, R. J. and O'Guinn, T. C. "Compulsive Consumption and Credit Abuse." *Journal of Consumer Policy* 11: 97-109.

120   Faber, R. J. and O'Guinn, T. C. "Classifying Compulsive Consumers: Advances in the Development of a Diagnostic Tool." In T. K. Srull, ed. *Advances in Consumer Research*. Provo, UT: Association of Consumer Research, 16, (1989) 738-744.

120   d'Astous, A. "An Inquiry into the Compulsive Side of Normal Consumers." *Journal of Consumer Policy* 13 (1990): 15-31.

120   *Ibid.*

121   Scherhorn, G. "The Addictive Trait in Buying Behavior." *Journal of Consumer Policy* 13 (1990): 33-51.

121   Faber, R. J. and O'Guinn, T. C. "Dysfunctional Consumer Socialization: A Search for the Roots of Compulsive Buying." Paper presented at the 13th Annual Colloquium of the International Association for Research in Economic Psychology, Leuven, Belgium, 1990.

124   Scherhorn. "The Addictive Trait in Buying Behavior." *Op. cit.*

127   Wright, J. "The Sneaky Things We Do to Hide Our Spending Habits." *Los Angeles Times* (November 27, 1992): E3-E5.

8. Will You Be My Mirror?

132   Theron, W., Nel, E. and Lubbe, A. "Relationship Between Body Image and Self-Consciousness." *Perceptual and Motor Skills* 73, no. 3, pt. 1 (1991): 979-983.

132   Miller, F. G., Davis, L. and Rowold, K. "Public Self-Consciousness, Social Anxiety, and Attitudes Toward the Use of Clothing." *Home Economics Research Journal* 10 (1982): 363-368.

133   Leary, M. and Kowolski, R. "Impression Management: A Literature Review and Two-Component Model." *Psychological Bulletin* 107, no. 1 (1990): 34-47.

133   Mori, D., Pliner, P. and Chaiken, S. "Eating Lightly and the Self-Presentation of Femininity." *Journal of Personality and Social Psychology* 53, no. 4 (1987): 693-702.

134   Larson, D. and Chastain, R. "Self-Concealment: Conceptualization, Measurement, and Health Implications." *Journal of Social and Clinical Pyschology* 9, no. 4 (1990): 439-455.

136   Baumgardner, A. H. "To Know Oneself Is to Like Oneself: Self-Certainty and Affect." *Journal of Personality and Social Psychology* 58, no. 6 (1990): 1062-1072.

136   Brockner, J. "Low Self-Esteem and Behavioral Plasticity: Some Implications." In L. Wheeler and P. Shaver, eds. *Review of Personality and Social Psychology*, vol. 4. Beverly Hills, CA: Sage, 1983, 237-271.

136   Baumgardner, A. H., Kaufman, C. M. and Levy, P. E. "Regulating Affect Interpersonally: When Low Esteem Leads to Greater Enhancement." *Journal of Personality and Social Psychology* 56 (1989): 907-921.

136   Baumeister, R. F., Tice, D. and Hutton, D. "Self-Presentational Interpretation of Personality Differences and Self-Esteem." Manuscript submitted for editorial review, Case Western Reserve University, Cleveland, Ohio, 1988.

136   Pelham, B. W. and Swann, W. B., Jr. "From Self-Conceptions to Self-Worth: On the Sources and Structure of Global Self-Esteem." *Journal of Personality and Social Psychology* 57 (1989): 672-680.

136   Swann, W. B., Jr. and Aron, J. Unpublished raw data, University of Texas at Austin, 1988.

137   Theron, *et al.* "Relationship Between Body Image and Self-Consciousness." *Op. cit.*

138   Schlenker, B. and Leary, M. "Social Anxiety and Communication About the Self." *Journal of Language and Social Psychology* 4, nos. 3 and 4 (1985): 171-192.

141   Wood, J. V. "Theory and Research Concerning Social Comparison of Personal Attributes." *Psychological Bulletin* 106 (1989): 231-249.

141   Wheeler, L. and Kunitate, M. "Social Comparison in Everyday Life." *Journal of Personality and Social Psychology* 62, no. 5 (1992): 760-773.

144   Buunk, B., Collins, R., Taylor, S. *et al.* "The Affective Consequences of Social Comparison: Either Direction Has Its Ups and Downs." *Journal of Personality and Social Psychology* 59, no. 6 (1990): 1238-1249.

145   Salovey, P. and Rodin, J. "Provoking Jealousy and Envy: Domain Relevance and Self-Esteem Threat." *Journal of Social and Clinical Psychology* 10, no. 4 (1991): 395-413.

145   Kenrick, D. T. and Gutierres, S. E. "Contrast Effects and Judgments of Physical Attractiveness: When Beauty Becomes a Social Problem." *Journal of Personality and Social Psychology* 38 (1980): 131-140.

149   Cohn, L. and Adler, N. "Female and Male Perceptions of Ideal Body Shape: Distorted Views Among Caucasian College Students." *Psychology of Women Quarterly* 16, no. 1 (March 1992): 69-76.

149   Douty, H. I. and Brannon, E. L. "Male and Female Preferences For Female Figures." *Home Economics Research Journal* 13 (1984): 122-137.

150   Thompson, J. K. and Tantleff, S. "Female and Male Ratings of Upper Torso: Actual, Ideal and Stereotypical Conceptions." *Journal of Social Behavior and Personality* 7 no. 2 (1992): 345-354.

150   Fallon, A. and Rozin, P. "Short Reports: Sex Differences in Perceptions of Desirable Body Shape." *Journal of Abnormal Psychology* 94, no. 1 (1985): 102-105.

150   Mathes, E. W., Brennan, S. M., Haugen, P. M. and Rice, H. B. "Ratings of Physical Attractiveness as a Function of Age." *Journal of Social Psychology* (1985): 157-168.

151   Heinberg, L. and Thompson, J. K. "Social Comparison: Gender, Target Importance Ratings, and Relation to Body Disturbance." *Journal of Social Behavior and Personality* 7, no. 2 (1992): 335-344.

153   Tannen. *You Just Don't Understand. Op. cit.*, Endnotes, Chapter 4.

9. If I Look Good, Will I Feel Good?

158   Darley, J. M. and Fazio, R. H. "Expectancy Confirmation Processes Arising in the Social Interaction Sequence." *American Psychologist* 35 (1980): 867-881.

158   Deaux, K. and Major, B. "Putting Gender Into Context: An Interactive Model of Gender-Related Behavior." *Psychological Review* 94 (1987): 369-389.

159   Miller, D. T. and Turnbull, W. "Expectancies and Interpersonal Processes." *Annual Review of Psychology* 37 (1986): 233-256.

159   Dion, K. L. "Stereotyping Based on Physical Attractiveness: Issues and Conceptual Perspective." In C. P. Herman, M. P. Zanna and E. T. Higgins, eds. *Appearance, Stigma, and Social*

Behavior: The Ontario Symposium on Personality and Social Psychology, vol. 3. Hillsdale, NJ: Erlbaum, 1986, 7-21.

159   Langlois, J. H. Contribution to *ibid.*

159   Taylor, G. S. and Spencer, B. A. "When Beauty Is the Beast." *Supervisory Management* (May 1989): 35-40.

159   Benson, P. L., Karabenck, S. A., and Lerner, R. M. "Pretty Pleases: The Effects of Physical Attractiveness, Race, and Sex on Receiving Help." *Journal of Experimental Social Psychology* 12 (1976): 409-415.

159   Fredricks, J. and Arenson, S. "Physical Attractiveness Stereotype in Causal Attributions for Socially Undesirable Behavior." *Psychological Reports* 70 (1992): 115-123.

160   Taylor "When Beauty Is the Beast." *Op. cit.*

160   Major, B. and Carnevale, P. "Physical Attractiveness and Self-Esteem: Attributions for Praise from an Other-Sex Evaluator." *Personality and Social Psychology Bulletin* 10, no. 1 (March 1984): 43-50.

160   Feingold, A. "Good-Looking People Are Not What We Think." *Psychological Bulletin* 111, no. 2: 304-341.

161   Canu, A. "Stereotypes About Physical and Social Characteristics Based on Social and Professional Competence Information." *Journal of Social Psychology* 13, no. 2 (1991): 225-231.

161   Feingold. "Good-Looking People Are Not What We Think." *Op. cit.*

162   Feingold, A. "Matching for Attractiveness in Romantic and Same-Sex Friends: A Meta-Analysis and Theoretical Critique." *Psychological Bulletin* 104 (1988): 226-235.

163   Branden, N. *How to Raise Your Self-Esteem.* New York: Bantam Books, 1987.

166   Roberts, J. E. and Monroe, S. "Vulnerable Self-Esteem and Depressive Symptoms: Prospective Findings Comparing Three Alternative Conceptualizations." *Journal of Personality and Social Psychology* 62, no. 5 (1992): 804-812.

167   Interview with Sandra Haber, Ph.D., quoted in Jacoby, "Self-Esteem You Can Have It Almost All the Time."

167   Westra, H. and Kuiper, N. "Type A, Irrational Cognitions, and Situational Factors Related to Stress." *Journal of Research in Personality* 26 (1992): 1-20.

167 Warren, L. W. and McEachren, L. "Derived Identity and Depressive Symptomatology Differing in Marital and Employment Status." *Psychology of Women Quarterly* 9, no. 1 (1985): 133-144.

167 Scarf, M. *Unfinished Business: Pressure Points in the Lives of Women.* New York: Doubleday, 1980.

174 Berscheid, E. and Walster, E. "Physical Attractiveness." In L. Berkowitz, ed. *Advances in Experimental Social Psychology*, vol. 17. New York: Academic Press, 1974, 157-215.

174 Nichter and Nichter. "Hype and Weight." *Op. cit.*, Endnotes, Chapter 3.

174 Goua, W., Ortega, S. and Style, C. "The Motivational and the Role Perspectives on Aging and Self Through the Adult Years: An Empirical Evaluation." *American Journal of Sociology* 9, no. 5 (March 1989): 1117-1145.

174 Chowdhary, U. "Self-Esteem, Age Identification, and Media Exposure of the Elderly and Their Relationship to Fashionability." *Clothing and Textiles Journal* 7 (Fall 1988): 23-30.

174 Pliner, P., Chaiken, S. and Flett, G. "Gender Differences in Concern with Body Weight and Physical Appearance Over the Life Span." *Personality and Social Psychology* 16, no. 2 (June 1990): 263-273.

174 Franzoi, S., Anderson, J. and Frommelt, S. "Individual Differences in Men's Perception of and Reactions to Thinning Hair." *The Journal of Social Psychology* 130, no. 2 (1989): 209-218.

175 Jerome, L. "Body Dysmorphic Disorder: A Controlled Study of Patients Requesting Rhinoplasty." *American Journal of Psychiatry* 149, no. 4 (April 1992): 377.

175 Better, N. M. "Dressing for Success? Try a Little Lifting and Tucking." *The New York Times* (May 26, 1992): A1(N), A1(L).

175 Marcus, P. "Psychological Aspects of Cosmetic Rhinoplasty." *British Journal of Plastic Surgery* 37 (1984): 313-318.

175 Jacobson, W. E., Edgerton, M. T., Meyer, E., et al. "Psychiatric Evaluation of Male Patients Seeking Plastic Surgery." *Plastic and Reconstructive Surgery* 26 (1969): 356-372.

175 Shipley, R., O'Donnell, J. and Bader, K. "Personality Characteristics of Women Seeking Breast Augmentation." *Plastic and Reconstructive Surgery* 60, no. 3 (1977): 369-376.

175 Schouten, J. "Selves in Transition: Symbolic Consumption in Personal Rites of Passage and Identity Reconstruction." *Journal of Consumer Research* 17 (March 1991): 412-425.

176 Schweitzer, I. "The Psychiatric Assessment of the Patient Requesting Facial Surgery." *Australian and New Zealand Journal of Psychiatry*, 23 (1989): 249-254.

177 Fraser, L. "The Cosmetic Surgery Hoax." *Glamour* (February 1990): 184, 185, 220-224.

10. Learning Appearance Security

182 Polhemus, T. *Body Styles*. Lutens, Netherlands: Lennard Publishing, 1988.

184 Thompson and Tantleff. "Female and Male Ratings of Upper Torso." *Op. cit.*, Endnotes, Chapter 8.

185 Interview with Rita Freedman, Ph.D. Cited in C. Sacra. "Mirrors: Why An Obsession With Your Reflection May Distort the Real You." *Health* (March 1990): 71-71, 90.

187 Strauman, T., Vookles, J., Berenstein, V. and Chaiken, S. "Self-Discrepancies and Vulnerability to Body Dissatisfaction and Disordered Eating." *Journal of Personality and Social Psychology* 61, no. 6 (1991): 946-956.

187 Noles, S. W., Cash, T. F. and Winstead, B. A. "Body Image, Physical Attractiveness, and Depression." *Journal of Consulting and Clinical Psychology* 53 (1985): 88-94.

187 Goleman, D. "When Ugliness Is Only in Your Eye, Body Image Can Reflect Mental Disturbance." *Time* (1992).

190 Salem, S. K. "Perceived Body Image, Importance of Ideal Body Image, Self-Esteem and Depression in Female College Students." *Dissertation Abstracts International* (1990): 1-20.

191 Gingus, J. "Body Image in Girls Pushes Rate of Depression Up." *APA Monitor* (October, 1989).

196 Rosen, J., Saltzburg, E. and Srebnick, D. "Cognitive Behavior Therapy for Negative Body Image." *Behavior Therapy* 20 (1989): 394-404.

11. Breaking The Cycle: Beyond Ourselves

202   Worsnop, R. L. "Eating Away at Themselves." *Dallas Morning News*, Health and Fitness Section (March 29, 1993): 4A, 4C.

202   Canning, H. and Mayer, J. "Obesity: An Analysis of Attitudes and Knowledge of Weight Control in Girls." *Research Quarterly* 39, (1967): 894-899.

203   Kennedy, D. B. and Homant, R. J. "Personnel Managers and the Stigmatized Employee." *Journal of Employment Counseling* 21 (1984): 89-94.

203   Karris, L. "Prejudice Against Obese Renters." *Journal of Social Psychology* 101 (1977): 159-160.

204   Allison, D. B., Basile, V. and Yuker, H. "The Measurement of Attitudes Toward and Beliefs About Obese Persons." *International Journal of Eating Disorders* 10, no. 5 (1991): 599-607.

206   Nichter and Nichter. "Hype and weight." *Op. cit.*, Endnotes, Chapter 3.

210   Personal interview with Norman Rauch, April 2, 1993.

RESOURCES

Self-Help Support Groups

Food Addicts Anonymous
P.O. Box 057394
W. Palm Beach, FL 33405
(407) 967-3871

Overeaters Anonymous
4025 Spencer St., Suite 203
Torrance, CA 90503
(213) 542-8363

Eating-Disorder Associations

National Anorexic Aid Society
5796 Karl Road
Columbus, OH 43229
(614) 436-1112

**ANAD — National Association
of Anorexia Nervosa and
Associated Disorders**
Box 7
Highland Park, IL 60035
(708) 831-3438

**ABC, Anorexia,
Bulimia Care, Inc.**
Box 213
Lincoln Center, MA 01733
(617) 257-9767

**American Anorexia/Bulimia
Association, Inc.**
133 Cedar Lane
Teaneck, NJ 07666
(201) 836-1800

**ANRED-Anorexia Nervosa and
Related Eating Disorders, Inc.**
P.O. Box 5102
Eugene, OR 97405
(503) 344-1144

**International Association of
Eating Disorder Professionals**
123 N.W. 13th Street, Suite 206
Boca Raton, FL 33432
(407) 338-6494

Social Activism/Information

**"The Facts About Weight
Loss Products and Programs"**
(free booklet)
Federal Trade Commission
Correspondence Branch
Washington, D.C. 20580

**National Association to Aid
Fat Americans**
P.O. Box 188620
Sacramento, CA 95818
(916) 443-0303

Questions About Steroid Abuse

Mr. Norman "Rocky" Rauch
P.O. Box 579
Lake Geneva, WI 53147
(414) 248-3105

Compulsive Exercise

There are currently no resources available that specifically target this problem. Many eating disorder resources address this as part of the eating disorder. For articles and information on athletes and overexercise write to:

National Collegiate Athletic Association
6201 College Blvd.
Overland Park, Kansas 66211-2422

Compulsive Shopping

Check in your local telephone directory for:

Debtor's Anonymous
(a 12-Step program that addresses compulsive spending)

Consumer Credit Counseling Service
(a non-profit organization that provides credit and financial counseling for individuals with financial difficulties)